US Department of
Transportation
**Research and
Special Programs
Administration**

I0438967

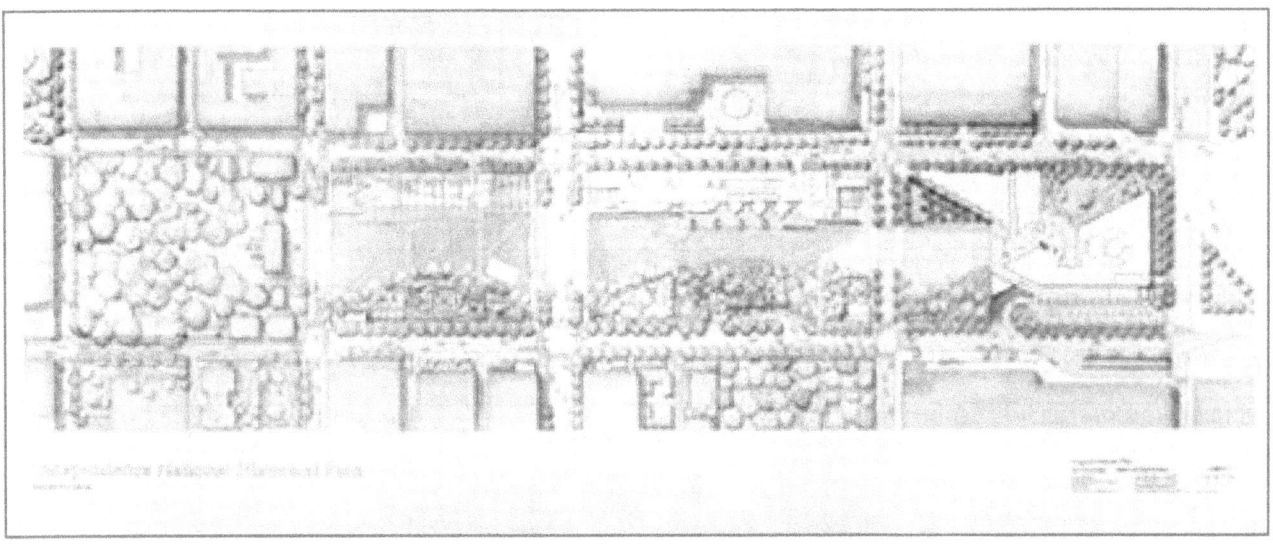

Evaluation of Bus Management Options
For
Independence National Historical Park

Final Report
July 6, 2000

Prepared for
**National Park Service
Northeast Region
200 Chestnut Street
Philadelphia, PA 19106**

Prepared by:
**John A. Volpe
National Transportation
Systems Center
Kendall Square
Cambridge, MA 02142**

REPORT DOCUMENTATION PAGE

1. REPORT DATE *(DD-MM-YYYY)*	2. REPORT TYPE	3. DATES COVERED *(From - To)*
07/2000	Planning Study	NA

4. TITLE AND SUBTITLE

Evaluation of Bus Management Options for Independence National Historical Site

5a. CONTRACT NUMBER
NA

5b. GRANT NUMBER
NA

5c. PROGRAM ELEMENT NUMBER
NA

6. AUTHOR(S)

David Spiller, Barry Mickela, Jeffrey R. Bryan

5d. PROJECT NUMBER

5e. TASK NUMBER
NPS TIC No. D-298

5f. WORK UNIT NUMBER
NA

7. PERFORMING ORGANIZATION NAME(S) AND ADDRESS(ES)

U.S. Department of Transportation
Research and Special Programs Administration
John A. Volpe National Transportation Systems Center

8. PERFORMING ORGANIZATION REPORT NUMBER

NA

9. SPONSORING/MONITORING AGENCY NAME(S) AND ADDRESS(ES)

National Park Service
Alternative Transportation Program
1201 Eye St. NW
Washington, DC 20005

10. SPONSOR/MONITOR'S ACRONYM(S)

WASO/ATP

11. SPONSOR/MONITOR'S REPORT NUMBER(S)

(see 5d. and 5e. above)

12. DISTRIBUTION/AVAILABILITY STATEMENT

Public distribution/availability.

13. SUPPLEMENTARY NOTES

This report addresses alternative transportation decision factors as indicated below (Y/N/NA):
(N) Non-construction options; (Y) park carrying capacity; (Y) life-cycle/ops. & maintenance costs; (Y) cost-effectiveness.

14. ABSTRACT

This project analyzes options and identifies preferred designs for a new transportation center in Independence National Historical Park. The Independence Transportation Center will be part of a planned National Constitution Center at Independence Mall. To determine the best type of facility, Volpe analyzed the consequences of each individual option, including capacity enhancement, safety, passenger quality, operational difficulty, impact on pedestrians, and visitor and environmental impacts. Capital and operational costs are discussed in detail before recommendations are presented.

15. SUBJECT TERMS

Independence National Historical Park, Alternative Transportation Facility, Bus parking capacity, Pedestrian and Environmental Impacts

16. SECURITY CLASSIFICATION OF:			17. LIMITATION OF ABSTRACT	18. NUMBER OF PAGES	19a. NAME OF RESPONSIBLE PERSON
a. REPORT	b. ABSTRACT	c. THIS PAGE	NA	96	Gary T. Ritter
None	None	None			19b. TELEPHONE NUMBER *(Include area code)* 617-494-2716, ritter@volpe.dot.gov

Reset

Table of Contents

1. Executive Summary

Independence Mall, which is part of Independence National Historical Park (INHP), is undergoing a major redevelopment. One key goal of the redevelopment is improved management of the numerous tour and school buses that bring visitors to the INHP; current estimates show that 24,750 buses arrive annually, bringing about 40% of the visitors to the Park. There is no existing bus management operation or facility for these vehicles, which can number over 60 per hour in peak season. Consequently, buses now ring the three-block Independence Mall, parked for the length of their visits, often with idling motors, creating a visual and auditory distraction for the Park visitor and a barrier for pedestrians.

A new National Constitution Center (NCC) building is a component of the intended development of the Mall. This new facility will be located on the northern end of Block 3 of the 3-block Mall. The NCC is designing and will develop and operate a museum focusing on the impact of the United States Constitution on the nation. In addition to designing the building itself, the NCC is responsible for the design and construction of the Independence Transportation Center (ITC), a bus facility that will service the entire Park. The NCC design team, led by architect Pei Cobb Freed and Partners (PCF&P), has developed a design for the bus facility. Orth-Rodgers Associates (ORA) has evaluated the ITC design for major problems and suggested improvements; they have also developed operational, enforcement, and marketing plans as components of the overall management of buses. The National Park Service (NPS) is responsible for design approval of the NCC design overall, including the proposed ITC and management plan

The National Park Service requested that the Volpe Center, of the U.S. Department of Transportation, provide an opinion on three bus facility and operation options that were being considered for INHP. During the initial analysis and review process three other options were proposed by the Volpe Center and the consultants working on INHP redevelopment projects. Each of the options are primarily located next to the proposed National Constitution Center (NCC) that will be built on Block 3 of Independence Mall. The six options[1] reviewed in this study are:

- Option 1: 11 saw tooth berths located on the eastern side of the NCC building and 3 saw tooth berths located in the DRPA "Bridge Triangle" property across Race Street, with overflow capacity on 5th Street. This option includes a 6-bus stacking area on Race Street.
- Option 2: A sub-grade facility under the NCC with 16 saw tooth berths and no overflow capacity.
- Option 3A: 16 saw tooth berths located on the eastern side of the NCC Building.
- Option 3B: 2 parallel berths on Race Street along the northern side of the NCC building, 11 saw tooth berths located on the eastern side of the building, and 3

---

[1] To the extent that any of these options require relocation of existing curbs and/or modification of existing cartway, city ordinance(s) may be required.

additional berths on the eastern edge of the bus facility. Overflow capacity of 5 berths is proposed on 6th Street, 3 opposite Block 3 and 2 opposite Block 1.

- Option 3C: 2 berths on Race Street, 11 saw tooth berths at NCC and 3 saw tooth berths in the DRPA Bridge Triangle. Entrance to the three DRPA Bridge Triangle berths is via a new driveway cut on the bridge ramp north of 5th Street.
- Option 4: 2 parallel berths along Race Street, 11 saw tooth berths on the eastern side of NCC, and 3 shallow saw tooth berths along the eastern edge of the bus facility. No overflow facility was mentioned in this option but is assumed to be on 5th Street.

For our evaluation, this report utilized the average daily count data and assumptions about peak seasons gathered by Orth Rodgers Associates (ORA). The current peak demand is on spring weekday afternoons when an estimated 64 buses arrive per hour between 12:00 to 1:30 P.M. Under current peak load bus arrival conditions, 16 bus berths at the primary facility appears to be a minimally sufficient number to reduce to a marginal impact the occurrence of overflow events. Under the projected bus arrival conditions of up to 85 buses per hour, the minimally sufficient number of bus berths is 21.

The Volpe Center believes the best design has both drop-off and pick-up berths for the ITC located in one central facility next to the NCC building, and not disbursed over a geographic area. This concept, however, is a difficult task to design within the footprint of the proposed NCC building and adjacent areas considering the existing and projected demand. Therefore,

- The Volpe Center proposes that at least all pick-ups occur in one location and that any overflow slots needed during peaks be used for drop-off only.
- Secondly, the Volpe Center agrees that in all options remote long-term parking be utilized. All three components: the primary facility, overflow spaces, and the remote parking need to be linked to work as a system. The mechanism for making this happen is a simplified bus management and operational control plan with a First Come First Serve system (FCFS).
- Thirdly, the dwell times for buses (especially for pick-up) will need to be prudently managed to achieve the optimal capacity cited above.
- Fourth, outreach and marketing efforts will need to be made to "flatten" the demand curve, reducing peak demand by spreading bus arrivals more evenly throughout the visiting day.
- Finally, regardless of which Option is selected, both the physical and operational management designs should be field tested in a full scale mock up, using large buses (e.g. 45 foot tour buses) and average drivers.

Option 1

Of the six options studied Option 1 is the most complex to manage. It requires that bus controllers stop each arriving bus at a stacking area on Race Street. This requirement for all buses to wait in the stacking area ensures that this area will be operating in overflow for most of the day during spring and fall weekdays. Since this area will be in overflow continuously, buses will be stopped on the exit ramp and on Race Street waiting to enter the stacking lanes. As drivers learn that this is a problem, more and more of them will probably find alternative places to drop off and/or pick up passengers, effectively undermining the operations plan. The Volpe Center recommends a simplified First Come First Serve system where the bus driver takes the first available berth without needing to stop in a stacking area.

The three DRPA Bridge Triangle berths are estimated to accommodate nine buses per hour. This means that the 14 total berths will actually function more like 12 berths, putting the system in overflow at demand above 40 bus arrivals per hour (with 10 minute average dwell time). The overflow spaces on 5th Street will pose a significant safety hazard to not only the buses, but to through traffic, as well. By putting 7 or 8 spaces along the east curb line between Market and Arch Streets, buses will have to parallel park to access these spaces. This very awkward maneuver is not appropriate for a city street. Proper design of these spaces requires a minimum length of 127 feet for each space to allow buses to enter and exit the spaces without parallel parking. Given the 400 feet available between Arch and Commerce Street this would allow for three bus turnouts.

Because loading zones will be separated between the NCC lot and the DRPA Bridge Triangle, inevitable problems will be encountered trying to direct passengers to the correct loading area. There are also safety concerns with passengers crossing Mid-block to and from the Triangle across busy Race Street.

Option 1 is not recommended for the above stated reasons.

Option 2

As designed, the underground bus facility does not take into account the fact that buses will be fueled by compressed natural gas (CNG).[2] A high release rate gas leak from a bus in the facility could create an explosion hazard. As the number of CNG fueled buses increases, there is a higher likelihood of a CNG-related incident occurring in the proposed underground bus facility. A prudent design must account for the operation of CNG fueled buses. The proposed design includes features that will make it difficult, at best, to incorporate recommended design provisions to mitigate the fire and explosion risk associated with CNG fueled buses. When handled properly and in a facility that is designed appropriately, CNG presents no greater risk than diesel fueled buses. To design and construct such a facility is estimated to cost $18,600,00.

The design also fails to consider the critical contingency of a disabled bus in one of the saw tooth bays that would require towing. A 45 foot tour bus requires a large, heavy-duty tow truck (approximately 30 ft. in length). The design proposes 16 bays around a central passenger loading and marshalling area, with buses circulating on the outside

---

[2] Although nearly all road coaches are now diesel fueled, that is changing. One out of four transit buses built today is CNG fueled, and as emissions standards are tightened, a significant percentage of road coaches will be CNG fueled, also. Liquefied Natural Gas (LNG) will not be widely used, so is not included in this report.

perimeter aisle. As many as three (3) turns are necessary to access a bus bay. There would be insufficient width in the aisle for a large tow truck to maneuver and establish a hookup with the disabled bus.

Option 2 is not recommended as the cost would be prohibitive to design and construct a facility that would adequately address these two safety issues.

Option 3A
The 16 berths of this option will satisfactorily meet demand 96% of the time under current peak bus arrivals. Option 3A allows the highest level of passenger safety and quality of service compared to the other options. Visitors to the Park are dropped off and picked up at a single location and can access the Park without crossing any streets containing through traffic.

An adverse impact of this design would be the encroachment into the landscaped area in the southwest corner of the NCC site, resulting from the expansion of the bus facility footprint. The bus turnout to 5th Street would be visible from the terrace and park areas, whereas in other options the bus facility would be shielded from view by the NCC structure. This can be mitigated through construction of a "designer" wall structure that would effectively provide separation.

This option clearly dominates on all technical evaluative criteria, except for the fact that it may violate an architectural/building line/view corridor constraint. To the extent this is an apparent "hard" site constraint it is recommended that Option 3A also be removed from further consideration.

Option 3B

In this option the three "overflow" spaces are northbound parking, with access to them provided by continuing the radius turn at the ITC exit ramp at the south end of the bus aisle. While not as simple as Option 3A, the operation of Option 3B is relatively straightforward. At the heart of this operational scheme is the FCFS regimen, which is favored by bus drivers, as it is perceived as the most fair to all. Buses arriving to drop off passengers will pull into the first available of the 11 berths along NCC. Once they are full then a bus controller can signal to the next buses to take the 2 berths on Race Street. If the berths on Race Street are occupied (or reserved for a known ADA requirement) during peak days, then the bus will turn into the ITC lot and the bus will return into the lot via the turnout at the south end and take the most forward open space of the 3. There will be Controllers located at both ends of the ITC bus aisle to direct bus movements and offer assistance when needed.

Under Option 3B, there is the potential for conflicting bus movements in the central aisle when a bus is backing out of the northern saw tooth berths simultaneous with a bus exiting the facility from one of the three quasi-overflow berths. In this situation for completely independent bus operations on both sides of the ITC, there would need to be 36 feet in the central aisle. With the current design, there is only 27 feet. The bus controller would, therefore, need to hold the buses backing out of the saw tooth berths when one of the three eastern berth buses was attempting to exit the facility. We also recommend that the sidewalk on the eastern edge of the ITC and passenger pickup area be at least 15 feet in width. This would require redesigning the facility or 5th Street to find an extra four feet.

Moving the stop line on Race Street back to the western edge of the ITC, which this option would require so as to allow the northbound buses to exit, does have a negative effect on the garage NCC exit. The garage entry/exit is too close to the existing stop line and could be blocked by queues of cards in any case under all the Options. Signage, with some enforcement, may be necessary to warn motorists not to proceed forward if they will block the entry/exit to the garage.

Another potential problem with this option is that it would necessitate a section of 12.75% grade, per the architect's newest drawing, at the return entrance into the south end of the ITC lot. Based on the configuration and bus dimensions, this grade presents a potential problem for buses returning into the lot when all saw tooth berths are full. Further analysis by Pennoni Associates, transportation engineers contracted by Pei Cobb Freed & Partners, shows that buses would have to depart on 6.2 percent downgrade and immediately enter on a 12.75 percent upgrade potentially creating a "roller coaster effect."

The Volpe Center made a scaled template of the design vehicle ("typical" 45 foot tour bus) and conducted simulated movements of a bus negotiating the ramp with the vertical road profile as indicated by the PCF drawings. While it is tight with respect to the approach, break over and departure angles of the vehicle, the bus can negotiate the ramp. For this reason, the Volpe Center recommends mitigation of the re-entry grade by use of a small embankment wall to separate the northern entry to the turnaround from the southern entry. Additionally, a guideline marking on the re-entry ramp to encourage buses to make the approach on a skewed angle will also effectively lower the re-entry grade. If both mitigation elements are in place, buses should not have a problem in negotiating the ramp.

If re-signalizing Race Street is not possible from the City's perspective, and all vehicles *must* exit the ITC facility onto 5th Street, then Option 3B would be removed from further consideration, and the next best alternative becomes Option 4,with the Volpe Center suggested design modifications included as listed below.

Option 3C

Option 3C nominally has 16 bus berths in the primary bus facility consisting of the three components and at three locations: the ITC, the three berths on the triangular island across Race Street, and the overflow berths on 5th Street. Each bus berth permits independent entry and exit, and would sustain an operation with no overflows 96% of the time under present bus arrival conditions during the peak. There will be some delay of passengers reaching the DRPA triangle for those three berths, which could decrease capacity due to increased bus dwell time.

Access to the 3 bus berths on the triangular island is via a new driveway cut off a major bridge/highway ramp. The Volpe Center is unaware of any other situation like this. Drivers' expectations are for a continuous flow on the bridge/highway ramp, and would be unprepared for a slowed vehicle making a left-turn into a driveway off the ramp. The situation is hazardous and could lead to a sizeable risk of rear-end collision. Slow buses turning left into the triangular island can lead to queues of following vehicles spilling back across the intersection of the bridge/highway ramp with Race Street.

The release of buses from the triangular island via the new driveway cut onto Race Street can lead to very serious problems. This is because buses under Option 3C are released at an uncontrolled, non-priority intersection (the intersection of the new driveway cut with Race Street). There can be substantial delays to a bus at the driveway cut attempting to turn onto Race Street. If the bus had completed a pass-by only through the triangular lot, and needed to cross two (2) lanes of traffic on Race Street in order to re-enter the ITC, the delay to the bus is even more substantial. Analysis of the delay to a bus at the release point for Option 3C shows it can lead to a catastrophic failure of interlocking queues.

Because of the potential safety problems with this design we recommend this Option be removed from further consideration.

Option 4

An earlier version of this option had been rejected in the early phases of preparation of this Report as unfeasible because of insufficient room in the central aisle for independent backing maneuvers of the buses from the forty five degree berths and the shallow saw tooth berths. Subsequent discussions with the City of Philadelphia yielded an increase in the dimension that could be utilized in the ITC design, gained by extending the existing 5th Street curb a total of 26'-4'' eastward from its existing location (i.e., 18'-4'' further east than the original proposal). The result is a central aisle width of approximately 29 feet. To have completely independent backing maneuvers, the central aisle would have to have approximately 39 feet from bumper to bumper of opposite parked buses.

In addition to this additional dimension, this option in order to work necessitated the incorporation of the following five design modifications, the first four of which are included in the current design for Option 4, and the fifth of which has resulted in an island platform dimension approximately 13 feet rather than the more optimum 15 feet:

- incorporation of a curb extension at 6th Street and Race to protect the "no thru traffic" lane which is the bus access lane to bus berths sited on the southern edge of Race Street;
- locating two (2), not three (3), bus berths, each of 90+ ft. and permitting independent entry and exit, on the southern edge of Race Street;

- adoption of the simplified bus management and control system with the FCFS regimen which would assure that the first 13 bus berths (2 on Race Street, and 11 adjacent to the NCC) are occupied first before the three (3) shallow saw-toothed overflow berths are utilized; and
- allocation of the additional 12 ft. primarily to the central bus aisle (11 ft for the central bus aisle, and 1 ft for the island platform on the eastern edge of the ITC, which brings the width of this platform to 11 ft. total); and
- redesigning the NCC walkway on the Western side of the ITC, next to the building or renegotiating with the City to find more space on 5th Street so the island platform on the eastern edge of the ITC can be at least 15 feet wide (e.g. finding four more feet).

The central aisle, even with these modifications, is still too narrow to permit complete independence of operations between the group of eleven (11) and the group of three (3) bus berths. There could be conflicting backing maneuvers. Some of these would occur with one or the other or both buses within the blind spot zone. Bus controllers would have to carefully control the operation.

Overflow facility

If the projected peak season, bus arrival conditions do materialize, an overflow facility will still have to be planned, designed and sited for five bus berths. This assumes that the preferred design option chosen now is either Option 3b, or Option 4 with 16 bus berths on site at the NCC. The Volpe Center strongly recommends that planning, design, and determination of a preferred site location are completed now (including the necessary Memoranda Of Understanding and political commitments to implement the facility). This would allow the overflow facility to come on-line before serious deterioration in the performance of the primary bus facility.

In reality, the only sensible site location(s) for the overflow facility is along one or more of the perimeter streets to the INHP. Other locations further away from the INHP would be inaccessible and inconvenient to passengers dropped off at the overflow facility who are destined for destinations contained within the INHP.

An overflow bus facility, consisting of a group of three (3) in-line bus turnouts and a group of two (2) in-line bus turnouts, is proposed to be sited opposite Block 3 and Block 1 respectively, on the western edge of 6th Street. The Volpe Center is aware of the political and value issues at stake in locating the overflow facility on 6th Street (or at a different location). These include the extensive routing that would be required for buses diverted from the primary bus facility to the overflow facility, neighbors not wanting a bus drop-off in front of their property, and reluctance on the part of the City and other constituencies to redesigning the street. There are technical issues concerned with displaced parking for cars, and mitigation needed. There are also security concerns of parking buses, even temporarily, in front of abutting Federal buildings.

For the short term, and perhaps on a permanent basis, the overflow facility will likely be on Block 2 of 5th Street between Arch and Commerce which can handle three berths. This location would only require overflow buses from the ITC to make a one block circuit. If the projected peak season bus arrival conditions do materialize, an overflow facility for five berths (two more then available on 5th Street, Block 2) will have to be planned, designed and located.

Costs

The Volpe Center believes that for the ITC to function properly, positions within the facility must be staffed by professionals who will be adequately compensated. A large percentage of visitors to the NCC and other parts of Independence Park will arrive on buses, and it is critical for the facility to operate smoothly and continue to refine operations to provide the most pleasant and efficient process possible. This policy is directly in line with the stated desire of NPS, NCC, and all other Mall stakeholders to provide a high quality experience for visitors to this important national treasure. The total annual salaries are estimated around $547,000. In addition to the staffing costs, there are other costs associated with operating the ITC facility. These costs can be broken down into equipment costs for installing the operating systems in the facility and annual equipment costs for maintenance, repair and replacement of equipment and other annual operating costs for items like cleaning, supplies, and similar requirements. The initial equipment cost is estimated at $263,000 with an annual cost of replacement and supplies at $65,000.

Option 3B design and construction costs are estimated to be $8.760,000 and Option 4 at $ 8,909,000.

2. Background

Independence Mall, which is part of Independence National Historical Park (INHP), is undergoing a major redevelopment. One key goal of the redevelopment is improved management of the numerous tour and school buses that bring visitors to the INHP; current estimates show that 24,750 buses arrive annually, bringing about 40% of the visitors to the Park. There is no existing bus management operation or facility for these vehicles, which can number over 60 per hour in peak season. Consequently, buses now ring the three-block Independence Mall, parked for the length of their visits creating a visual and auditory distraction for the Park visitor and a barrier for pedestrians.

A new National Constitution Center (NCC) building is a component of the intended development of the Mall. This new facility will be located on the northern end of Block 3 of the 3-block Mall. The NCC is designing and will develop and operate a museum focusing on the impact of the United States Constitution on the nation. In addition to designing the building itself, the NCC is responsible for the design and construction of the Independence Transportation Center (ITC), a bus facility that will service the entire Park. The NCC design team, led by architect Pei Cobb Freed and Partners (PCF&P), has developed a design for the bus facility. Orth-Rodgers Associates (ORA) has evaluated the ITC design for major problems and suggested improvements; they have also developed operational, enforcement, and marketing plans as components of the overall management of buses. The National Park Service (NPS) is responsible for design approval of the NCC design overall, including the proposed ITC and management plan.

The National Park Service requested that the Volpe Center provide a second opinion of the ORA study. In particular, the request was to evaluate the accuracy of the study's review of the PCF&P schematic design and the validity of its associated management plan. In addition the Volpe Center has evaluated the proposed design against other design alternatives either previously considered or those that emerged during the course of this study.

This report outlines the Volpe Center findings for six (6) bus facility designs:

- Option 1: The ORA recommended design of 11 saw tooth berths located on the eastern side of the NCC building and 3 saw tooth berths located in the DRPA "Bridge Triangle" property across Race Street, with overflow capacity on 5th Street. This option includes a 6-bus stacking area on Race Street.
- Option 2: A sub-grade facility with 16 saw tooth berths and no overflow capacity.
- Option 3A: 16 saw tooth berths located on the eastern side of the NCC Building.
- Option 3B: 2 parallel berths on Race Street along the northern side of the NCC building, 11 saw tooth berths located on the eastern side of the building, and 3 additional berths on the eastern edge of the bus facility. Overflow capacity of five berths is proposed on 6th Street, three opposite Block 3 and two opposite Block 1.
- Option 3C: A revised plan by ORA that includes 2 berths on Race Street, 11 saw tooth berths at NCC and 3 saw tooth berths in the DRPA Bridge Triangle.

Entrance to the three DRPA Bridge Triangle berths is via a new driveway cut on the bridge ramp north of 5th Street.

- Option 4: A revised PCF&P option with two parallel berths along Race Street, 11 saw tooth berths on the eastern side of NCC, and three shallow saw tooth berths along the eastern edge of the bus facility. No overflow facility was mentioned in this option.

All of the design Options evaluated in this report will require moving the sidewalk along the eastern edge of the ITC and involve a change to the current traffic patterns. Therefore, a City ordinance will be required before any final plan can be approved.

For each of the options the Volpe Center team applied seven criteria for the evaluation:

- capacity of the option to meet current and projected demands;
- safety for the bus passenger;
- passenger quality of service;
- operational complexity;
- capital and operational costs;
- pedestrian impact and
- visitor and environmental impacts.

2.1. General Findings

As the Volpe Center team examined each of the five options and after two site visits, several themes emerged that are consistent regardless of the final option chosen. These themes relate to capacity needs for current and future demand, a general preferred concept, a preferred concept of operation, routing of buses to the facility and to overflow drop-offs, and marketing to tour bus operators and school systems. These themes are discussed below.

2.1.1. Capacity Needs

The Volpe Center utilized the average daily count data and assumptions about peak seasons gathered by Orth Rodgers for our evaluations. It is understood that the field survey data was limited to two spring school days, one spring holiday, and one summer Saturday. The data, because of the limited sampling, may therefore under or overestimate actual peak demand.[3] Nonetheless, the current peak demand is on spring weekday afternoons when an estimated 64 buses arrive per hour between 12:00 to 1:30 P.M. The majority of these buses would be picking up passengers and likely be on tight schedules either to return to a school or to another tour destination.

In addition to field observations of on-street bus accumulation in both loading and unloading modes, Orth-Rodgers and Associates (ORA), the traffic and site-engineering consultants, used an analytical queuing model to determine needed capacity for the bus

---

[3] Although sampling was limited, ORA believes the data represents a peak day. Average weekday Liberty Bell attendance in spring 1998 was 5,500. Attendance on the sample day was 9,288. Limited field observations on other days suggest that the survey data is representative of high bus activity.

facility. The model, described briefly in their response to the city of Philadelphia's Request for Proposals for a Bus Management Study, assumes multiple servers, random bus arrivals, and exponentially distributed service times relative to an average dwell time. This is formally known as an M/M/N queuing system, and is a suitable model for this type of application.

An essential component of evaluating the size or capacity of the bus facility, specifically responding to the question of how many bus berths are required, is the probability of overflow. This is the probability that one or more buses arrive during a time when all the berths are occupied or busy. The probability of an overflow is equivalent to the probability that one or more buses have to wait in queue. These buses wait to either be served by the primary bus facility or divert to an overflow facility. The probability of an overflow has been calculated as a function of average dwell time (8-15 minutes), the number of bus berths, and the average bus arrival rate (see Appendix B).

The Volpe Center used the average dwell time of 10 minutes to calculate the probability of an overflow for each option studied. For drop-offs, 10 minutes is more than sufficient, and, on average, this dwell time is adequate for pick-ups. Under current peak load bus arrival conditions, 16 bus berths at the primary facility appears to be a minimally sufficient number to reduce to a marginal impact the occurrence of overflow events. Under the projected bus arrival conditions of up to 85 buses per hour, this number of berths (N=16) fails. To obtain a near equivalent performance (i.e., minimal overflow events), the minimally sufficient number of bus berths for an arrival rate of 85 buses per hour is 21. If the projected peak season bus arrival conditions do materialize, an overflow facility for five berths will have to be planned, designed and located. 5th Street between Market and Arch Streets has been proposed already, while the Volpe Center believes a more suitable site is 6th Street, with three berths opposite Block 3 and 2 berths opposite Block 1.

2.1.2. Overall Preferred Concept

The Volpe Center believes the best design has both drop-off and pick-up berths located in one central facility next to the NCC building, and not disbursed over a geographic area. A primary facility ensures less passenger confusion about where to congregate for pick up, provides additional safety and protection from inclement weather and simplifies bus operations. This concept, however, is a difficult task to design within the footprint of the proposed NCC building and adjacent areas considering the existing and projected demand. Therefore, The Volpe Center proposes that at least all pick-ups occur in one location and that any overflow slots needed during peaks be used for drop-off only. Secondly, the Volpe Center agrees that in all options remote long-term parking be utilized. This site should be reasonably accessible to both the primary bus facility and the overflow facility, with designated routings (minimizing environmental impacts on neighborhoods) established between the latter sites and the long term parking facility. All three components: the primary facility, overflow spaces, and the remote parking need to be linked to work as a system. The mechanism for making this happen is a simplified bus management and operational control plan. Thirdly, the dwell times for buses (especially for pick-up) will need to be prudently managed to achieve the optimal capacity cited above. Finally, outreach and marketing efforts will need to be made to "flatten" the demand curve, reducing peak demand by spreading bus arrivals more evenly throughout the visiting day.

2.1.3. Preferred Concept of Operation

A bus operation refers to managing the orderly arrival and departure of buses through the ITC and, if needed, to the overflow facility; this includes both unloading and loading cycles. The operation plan should take into account the safety and convenience of passengers as well as a clear set of rules for bus drivers and the ITC staff.

The preferred objective is a decentralized and autonomous management and control system utilizing a set of simple, enforceable rules that each individual bus driver can follow. The system performance of the combined primary bus facility and the overflow facility needs to be efficient, effective, and safe.

The Volpe Center recommends no advanced scheduling and assignment of bus bays. Rather, bus drivers arriving to drop off passengers should follow a First Come First Served (FCFS) regimen and will be instructed to dock at the first available (empty) bus berth in the primary bus facility. Bus bay assignments are dynamically assigned in real time. Importantly, the individual driver makes this decision by adhering to this rule. Drivers, companies, and on-board arriving passengers will perceive the FCFS regimen as equitable and understandable. In the event that all bus berths are occupied, bus drivers will be instructed to not queue in the bus aisle, but to immediately exit the ITC and follow the designated routing to the overflow facility. In the very rare instance (non-existent under current peak demand) that the overflow facility bus turnouts are also all occupied, bus drivers will be instructed to follow a designated return routing back to the primary bus facility and repeat the cycle. When buses stop in berths, greeters take information from the drivers or tour leaders (name of tour group, approximate time of pick up, etc.) and assign a number to each bus; all information is entered into an electronic databank system. A numbered sign is given to the bus operator that is displayed in the bus front glass to identify the bus on its return to pick up passengers.

All pick-ups should be made at the primary bus facility. The reason for this is to eliminate any confusion as to multiple pick-up sites. This rule allows passenger groups to be efficiently marshaled to arrive at the pick-up location before the expected time of arrival (ETA) of the group's bus. This will help reduce loading dwell time. No advanced scheduling or reservation of bus berths for pick-ups is allowed. Each bus driver (jointly with his group leader) will determine his own ETA for pick-up. Bus drivers will follow a FCFS regimen and will be instructed to dock at the first available (empty) bus berth. Bus drivers will be instructed to not queue in the bus aisle, but to immediately exit the primary bus facility and follow the designated routing for a "go-around" (analogous to a holding pattern for an aircraft) in the event that all bus berths are occupied. Bus drivers will repeat this cycle until they can dock at a bus berth for pick-up at the primary bus facility. As soon as the berth is known for a particular bus, a controller or greeter enters the bus number and berth into the database. A passenger display system (video, audio, and handheld messaging device for the greeters) announces bus arrivals. The announcement system broadcasts and displays the group name and berth location – now ready for immediate boarding. Hand held devices used by the greeters and controllers would allow entry and retrieval of bus information in real time.

2.1.4. Routing

The Volpe Center agrees with the NPS and NCC recommendation to route eastbound buses off Route 676 to exit at Eighth Street. This will allow ample distance over two to three blocks for buses to get into the right hand lane on Race Street to then enter the bus facility. Westbound buses from 676 or I-95 will still need to get off at the Sixth Street exit and make the left onto Race Street; while not as preferable as the 8th Street exit, the 6th Street exit should be adequate.

2.1.5. Marketing

The Volpe Center agrees with the ORA Bus Management Plan that even with the simplest bus operation it will be necessary to develop an information "campaign" for the tour bus operators and school groups. Drivers need to know how the bus facility will operate, where the overflow berths are located, and routing to the remote parking. In addition, it would be helpful for tour leaders and school groups to know when the peak demand is anticipated so they can plan accordingly. As recommended by ORA, the marketing effort should be an integral part of the overall marketing plan and public information activities of the different agencies and visitor attractions.

Specific findings of the analysis of the six options follow in sections 2.2 through 2.7.

2.2. Option 1

2.2.1. Overview

The bus facility described under Option 1 was designed within the constraints set by the Independence Mall master planner (Olin Partnership), the NCC, and its architect Pei Cobb Freed. Abrams-Cherwony & Associates, as sub-consultants to ORA, subsequently developed a bus management plan using traffic data compiled by Orth Rodgers. The option 1 configuration includes 11 saw tooth berths located on the eastern side of the NCC building, 3 saw tooth berths located in the DRPA Bridge Triangle property across Race Street, 3 curbside spaces on Race Street between 6th Street and the entrance to the NCC underground parking garage, 3 spaces on Race Street parallel to these three curbside spaces (dedicated for bus use only) and an overflow site with 7 or 8 spaces on 5th Street between Market and Arch Streets. The curbside Race Street spaces are for stacking and loading/unloading and the adjacent three spaces are for stacking only.

Figure 2.2.1 shows the arrangement of the fourteen saw tooth spaces located at the NCC building and in the DRPA Bridge Triangle. To accommodate overflow conditions, that is, when the bus arrival rate exceeds capacity at the facility, this option proposes 7 or 8 overflow berths on 5th Street, between Market and Arch Streets.

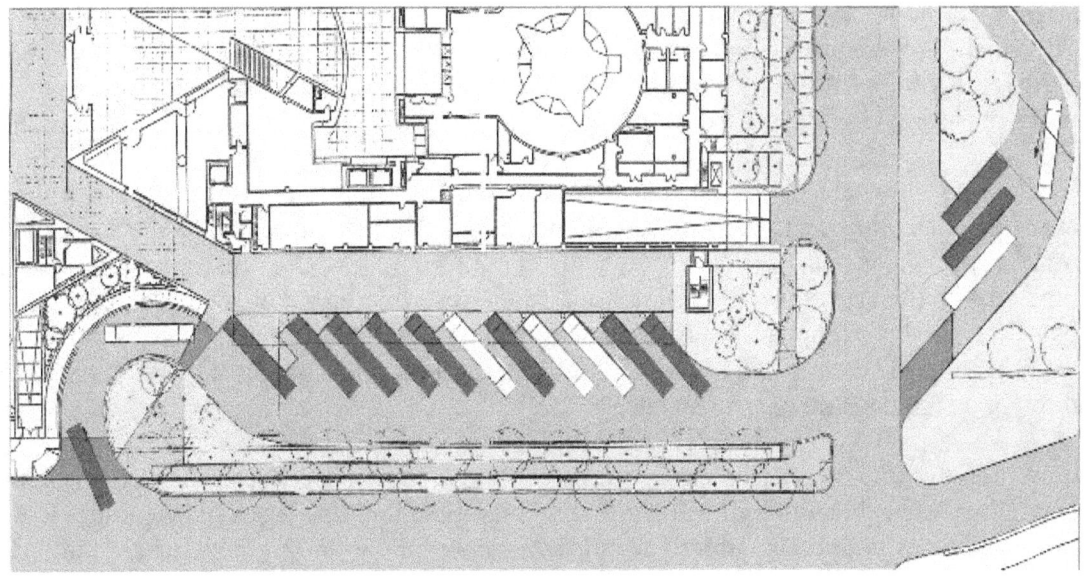

Figure 2.2.1. Option 1 - Saw Tooth Berth Arrangement

2.2.2. Capacity

Assuming a 10-minute average dwell time[4] for loading and unloading passengers, ORA estimates that Option 1 has a capacity of 46 buses per hour. This estimate assumes that

---

[4] 10 minutes is probably high for unloading operations and possibly low for loading operations, but it provides a good starting point for comparison of the different options. A primary focus in the future,

the 11 NCC saw tooth berths will be used for loading and unloading, and the three DRPA Bridge Triangle spaces will be used for loading and scheduled unloading. The bus and traffic counts done by ORA indicate that the only time bus arrivals exceed the capacity of this option, necessitating use of the overflow berths, is during spring weekdays, which comprise 18% of total visitation days at the park. On these days, the overflow berths would be needed between 10:00 – 11:00 A.M. and 12:00 – 1:30 P.M. Future bus arrival rates have been estimated to be 30% higher than current rates, but this number is an estimate only. Under this scenario, fall weekdays (17% of total visitation days) would see an overflow condition between 10:00 – 11:00 A.M. and 12:00 – 1:30 P.M. These future estimates could be revised through prudent management of the ITC, including taking steps to minimize dwell times and outreaching to school and tour groups to schedule arrivals to flatten the peak arrival rates and spread them throughout the day.

The estimates of Option 1 capacity, however, appear to be overly optimistic, based on the operational plan associated with this option, which calls for each bus to first access the stacking area on Race Street (see Figure 2.2.2 on the following page) before proceeding to a saw tooth berth, unless pre-authorized by a bus controller or the ITC manager to proceed directly to a berth. The operational complexity of this option is discussed in detail in Section 2.2.5. The three DRPA Bridge Triangle spaces are estimated to accommodate nine buses per hour by the proposers. This means that the 14 berths will actually function like 12 berths, putting the system in overflow at demand above 40 bus arrivals per hour (with 10 minute average dwell time). Since actual dwell times for drop off will be significantly shorter than for pick up (e.g. 8 minute dwell time), the "12" berths will likely handle most drop offs under current demand, except during morning peaks on spring weekdays (10-11:00 A.M.).

Because all buses are required under this option to first stop at the Race Street stacking area, that area will be in overflow condition virtually 100% of the time, as there are only 6 total spaces that, due to the layout, will function more like 2 at best. Even at dwell times as low as 1 minute for information gathering, this area will continuously be in overflow. A bus stopped in the first outer stacking space will block all buses behind it from leaving the area. This stacking area configuration will have an adverse impact on through traffic on Race and 6th Streets.

The 7 or 8 overflow spaces on 5th Street will not function properly during overload conditions. This layout requires parallel parking operations for buses pulling into or out of these spaces on the city street. To allow for appropriate turning movements into and out of a curbside space in through traffic conditions at 20 mph, a minimum of 175 feet is needed for a 45-foot bus. Therefore, a maximum of two overflow spaces can fit into the proposed 5th Street area. From the existing bus arrival numbers, the overflow spaces will be full, necessitating drivers to fend for themselves more than 12 % of the time during spring weekdays between 12:00 – 1:30 P.M., as overflow of these spaces is not addressed in the operations plan.

---

regardless of the Option selected, should be for the ITC management and staff to work closely with bus groups to minimize all dwell times.

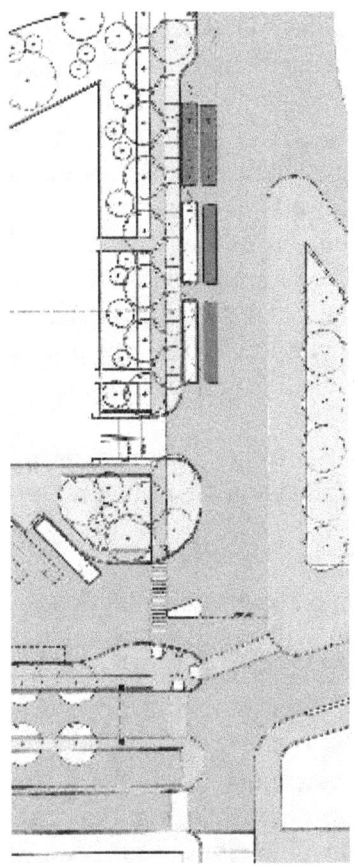

Figure 2.2.2 Option 1 - Stacking Spaces for six Buses on Race St.

2.2.3. Safety

Buses are assumed by the ORA operation plan to be entering Race Street from the 6th Street highway exit[5]. This requires buses to cross both lanes of Race Street traffic to get into the stacking area in a short distance. Since this area will be in overflow continuously, buses will be stopped on the exit ramp and on Race Street waiting to enter the stacking lanes. As drivers learn that this is a problem, more and more of them will probably find alternative places to drop off and/or pick up passengers, effectively undermining the operations plan.

Passengers arriving or leaving from buses in the three DRPA Bridge Triangle berths must cross Race Street as well as bus traffic into NCC and out of the DRPA Bridge Triangle berths. Since these spaces are not co-located with the others, there will be occurrences of "lost" passengers darting across Race Street. Passengers could easily cross Race Street mid-block to save walking time to access the crosswalk and signal at Race and 5th Streets. There would have to be pedestrian fences installed along the front of the 3 bus berths in

---

[5] Regardless of the option selected, signage should direct westbound buses off Route 676 to exit on the 8th Street ramp, and then proceed east on Race Street to the facility. Eastbound buses from 676 or I-95 need to get off at the 6th Street exit.

19

the triangular island, and along the island separating the ITC adjacent to the NCC from 5th Street. These would prevent inadvertent slipping into Race Street and 5th Street into oncoming traffic.

The overflow spaces on 5th Street will pose a significant safety hazard to not only the buses, but to through traffic as well. By putting 7 or 8 spaces along the east curb line between Market and Arch Streets, buses will have to parallel park to access these spaces. This very awkward maneuver is not appropriate for a city street. Proper design of these spaces requires a <u>minimum</u> length of 127 feet for each space to allow buses to enter and exit the spaces without parallel parking. Given the 400 feet available between Arch and Commerce Street this would allow for three bus turnouts.

Buses arriving at the three DRPA Bridge Triangle berths that find those berths occupied pose a safety hazard by being stopped on the bridge ramp area and Race Street.

2.2.4. Passenger Quality of Service

Virtually all passengers arriving on buses will experience delays and traffic problems due to the overflow conditions that will result from having all buses stop at the stacking spaces on Race Street. Many drivers will be forced to drive past the facility and then work their way back via several turns, due to the one-way patterns present in the area of the NCC. Passengers who have spent several hours on buses could find this very upsetting. If all saw tooth berths are occupied after a bus has cleared the stacking lanes, the bus will again be held, or stacked, along Race Street. Passengers will thus be required to twice sit on the bus within sight of the NCC. Many of these passengers may need restroom facilities or other considerations, especially after a long bus ride.

Passengers who are required to load or unload at the DRPA Bridge Triangle berths will walk past the saw tooth berths, and they will wonder why they had to load or unload offsite and then walk to/from the NCC. This will especially be a problem on rainy days.

On spring weekdays, more than 10% of bus passengers will be routed to the overflow spaces on 5th Street, where the buses will experience problems parking. These passengers will then cross 5th Street in the process to get to the NCC, Visitor Center or Independence Hall.

Because loading zones will be separated, inevitable problems will be encountered trying to direct passengers to the correct loading area.

For passengers arriving at the Mall by bus, the visitation to which currently is estimated at 1.25 million annually to the NCC alone, the facility where they unload and are picked up will be their first and last image of Independence Park. It is imperative that this experience be designed to enhance, and not detract from, the overall visitation experience. Option 1 will not accomplish this for existing peak times on spring weekdays, which means that more than 80,000 annual visitors will experience overflow conditions at best, if the option works as proposed. The number of visitors that will actually be inconvenienced is likely to be significantly higher, estimated to be 130,000 passengers, since it is believed that option 1 will not function as proposed. This means that at least 10% of all visitors to Independence NHP will experience some form of inconvenience arriving and/or leaving.

Similar to the other five alternatives under consideration, Option 1 would provide the majority of visitors with convenient and safe access to Independence NHP, thus enhancing the quality of experience enjoyed by visitors. This would not be the case, however, for those arriving by bus at the three berths in the triangular island lot across Race Street. These visitors would encounter some disadvantages:

- Crossing heavy traffic on Race Street would be less convenient and potentially less safe than access from the main parking lot adjacent to the NCC.
- Passengers scheduled for pick up at berths in this small lot may have to wait outside for the actual bus arrival, sometimes in inclement weather. A canopy at the island berths would provide some relief.

In addition, for all visitors arriving by bus, the scheduling information to be collected from bus drivers before entering parking areas would result in stacking of buses on Race Street, causing delays and inconvenience for passengers.

2.2.5. Operational Complexity

Of the six options studied, Option 1 is the most complicated to manage. It requires that bus controllers stop each arriving bus at the stacking area on Race Street. The purpose of the stacking is for the bus controller to talk with each bus driver to
- determine if a lift is needed form the remote parking area;
- give directions to the driver before passengers disembark so the driver can direst his passengers; and/or
- hold a bus when a controller knows a berth will be free momentarily

Given the requirement for all buses to wait in the stacking area ensures that this area will be operating in overflow for most of the day during spring and fall weekdays. This will place a heavy burden on the bus controllers to move buses into and out of the stacking lanes as quickly as possible. The buses in the three curbside spaces and the buses in the middle and rear outside spaces will essentially be trapped by the bus stopped in the front outside space. Anything that happens to delay the front outside bus will prevent the other five buses from proceeding to a berth as directed by a controller. Holding buses here to gather information will exacerbate the problems.

It is planned that the bus controllers will meet each incoming bus at the stacking area, and hold the bus there to obtain information from the driver. The controllers will then instruct the drivers to proceed to specific berths at the NCC facility. If all saw tooth berths are occupied, the buses will be stacked along Race Street awaiting open berths. This will require a second controller location, to again instruct buses to proceed to open berths. A third controller station would be in the ITC lot to assist buses into and out of saw tooth berths. All controllers will have to be in constant communication, relaying information on buses and berths. Controllers at the stacking lanes must know if all berths and the stacking lane along Race Street are full, in order to direct buses to the 5th Street overflow spaces, which will require a fourth controller location. The staffing plan prepared for Option 1 does not include enough controllers to accomplish this complicated control of bus movements.

The three DRPA Bridge Triangle berths would not be available for unloading, since they are not accessible once a bus has entered the stacking lanes. This reduces their effectiveness considerably. Attempting to schedule bus arrivals at these berths will not function as planned, due to traffic and other delays that will inevitably occur. If the controllers schedule three buses to arrive at a specific time and three others to arrive 20 minutes later[6] in the anticipation that the first three will have departed, there will be occasions when all six buses show up at the same time. There is no room to accommodate buses stacking at the DRPA Bridge Triangle, so these buses will either have to exit the DRPA Bridge Triangle without stopping or stack up in traffic flow areas. This will require a fifth controller location, as well, to take information from scheduled arrivals and direct traffic through the DRPA Bridge Triangle.

Attempting to pre-arrange where arriving buses will unload passengers (or pick up passengers) will lead to inevitable conflicts. Available berths will sit unoccupied when buses are late, which reduces the overall capacity of the facility considerably. Buses that are delayed by traffic or other reasons will arrive to find their assigned berths occupied. Unless there is a controller present to help alleviate problems with these situations, bus drivers will have to fend for themselves, similar to the current situation without an ITC facility, and will begin dropping off passengers wherever it is most convenient to them, effectively undermining the operation.

Controllers are proposed to collect information from the drivers, but this function would be better performed by the Greeters, who meet with the buses at each of the locations. Greeters can input the collected information into the system.

This option recognizes that the staffing level of the ITC will vary by season, with additional staff required for peak times. However, it underestimates the numbers and skill levels necessary for each position description.

2.2.6. Impact on Pedestrians

Pedestrians walking north on 5th Street will have to cross bus traffic exiting the ITC, but this is true of all of the options except 3A. Option 1 affords ample pedestrian capability on 5th Street. If the curbside stacking spaces on Race Street are used to unload passengers, as proposed during slow periods, pedestrians on the south side of Race Street will need to negotiate through tour groups milling on the sidewalk there, but the sidewalk is more than ample to accommodate this. Pedestrians walking on the east side of 5th Street will have to deal with overflow buses between Market and Arch Streets. While all overflow areas will have pedestrian impact, the proposed 7 or 8 spaces could put up to 400 bus passengers on the sidewalk at the same time, which would seriously impede pedestrians walking up 5th Street.

---

[6] The Option 1 plan calls for 9 buses per hour usage at these 3 berths, or 1 every 20 minutes per berth.

2.2.7. Visitor and Environmental Impacts

Option 1 stops buses at the stacking area and along Race Street if all saw tooth berths are full before their entering the ITC lot. This means that increased tailpipe emissions will be present as compared to other options.

Common to all the options, the consolidation of bus operations at the northern end of INHP would reduce bus parking and circulation on 6th Street and most of 5th Street. As a result, the pedestrian environment would be improved surrounding much of the park in the immediate vicinity of adjacent commercial and institutional land uses.

When buses need to be diverted to the triangular lot across Race Street after first attempting to find available space in the primary lot, there will be increased circulation on nearby streets, including 4th, Arch, and 7th Streets, reducing the beneficial effects on land use associated with concentrating bus operations on Race Street. While in the future bus overflow conditions are anticipated in periods of peak demand, even when both lots are fully occupied this option will not differ appreciably from the others in terms of the amount of increased bus circulation that will occur on nearby streets.

If future demand forecasts prove to be accurate, additional spaces will be needed for loading and unloading a number of buses during periods of peak visitation. Potential locations for these loading/unloading spaces are on 5th and 6th Streets. A variety of constraints limits the locations available for locating these spaces. Security regulations preclude the use of curb areas adjacent to the U.S Mint on 5th Street and the U.S. Courthouse on 6th Street. NPS recognizes the significant level of completed, ongoing and contemplated property improvements and expansion around the perimeter of the Mall and does not wish to continue separating these properties from the Mall by a wall of buses. Nevertheless, as described in other sections of this report, there appears to be space for 1 loading/unloading area on 5th Street and 2 areas on 6th Street. Use of these spaces would be seasonal and relatively infrequent. Moreover, pedestrian safety could be enhanced through design treatments at the overflow berths such as raising crosswalks for the purpose of "traffic calming' (see chapter 3 for a fuller description). The Volpe Center understands that this enhancement option may be difficult to achieve due to concerns cited by the City Traffic Department and because 5th and 6th Streets are designated state highways.

The bus facility adjacent to the NCC would be relatively unobtrusive to the Park vistor. Design treatments, such as lowering the pavement of the bus berths and landscaping along 5th Street, can mitigate any visual impacts.

2.3. Option 2

2.3.1. Overview

This option proposes a sub-grade ITC bus facility, within the footprint of the NCC structure. The bus facility would be sited at the lowest level (B3), possibly with additional car parking as well. Bus berths would be sited around a central passenger marshalling and loading/unloading platform. Buses would circulate in a perimeter aisle to access the individual bus berths. Entry and exit to/from the berths would be from/to this central aisle. Access by buses to the facility is via a series of down and up ramps. Entry and exit to the ITC facility is on Race Street.

The spatial configuration of the bus berths is U-shaped, consisting of 4-8-4 berths respectively along the three sides of the central platform. As many as three turns would be necessary to access bus berth #13, #14, #15 and #16 (see Figure 2.3.1). Access by passengers, between the upper floors of the NCC structure and the central platform, to the loading/unloading zone is by a combined escalator and stairway. One elevator is also provided for the elderly and the mobility-impaired.

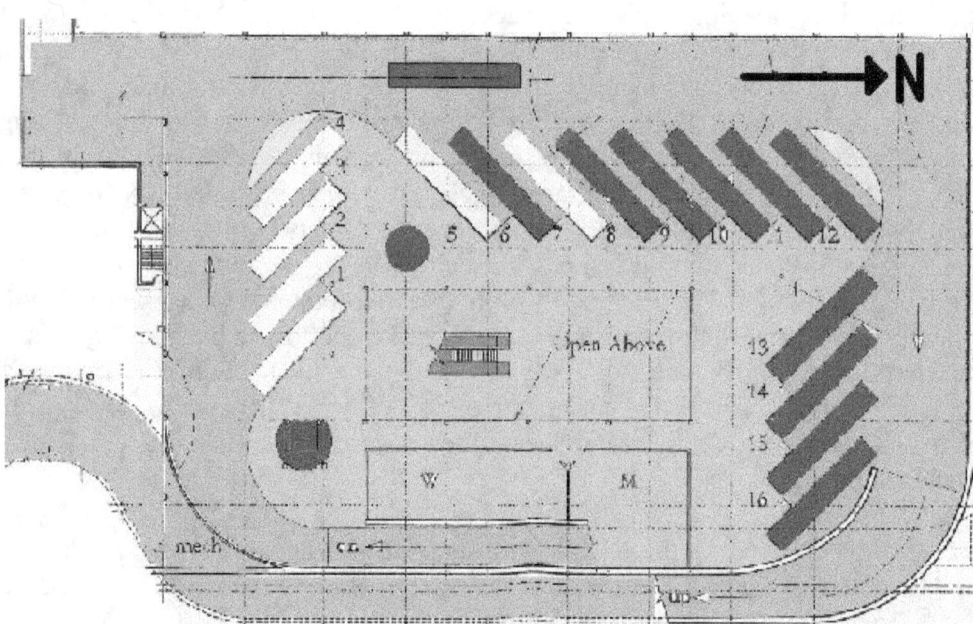

Figure 2.3.1 Option 2 – 16 Saw Tooth Berth Arrangement in Underground Facility

2.3.2. Capacity

The proposed sub-grade ITC bus facility is sized at sixteen (16) berths. No overflow facility has been proposed for this option, although presumably the intended overflow facility on 5th Street to service Option 1 would also have been available for this option. The Volpe Center concerns related to the proposed utilization of the space on 5th Street for buses loading and unloading during overflow conditions, however, are still germane.

The space constraints on locating bus berths opposite Block 2, between Market Street and Commerce Street, permit at best 2 well-designed bus turnouts. The overflow facility on 5th Street for Option 1 that might also be used for Option 2 intended a bumper-to-bumper stacking of up to 7 buses. Independent entry and exit under these conditions would not be possible.

Under current peak conditions for bus arrivals, 16 berths are adequate. Overflow conditions are likely only 4 percent of the time, assuming approximately 60 buses arrive per hour, and with an assumed average dwell time per bus of 10 minutes (see Appendix B).

Under projected levels for bus arrivals (e.g., > 80 buses per hour), however, the likelihood for an overflow condition (i.e., one or more buses arrive when all sixteen (16) bus berths are occupied) rises to 32 percent under the same assumptions with respect to average bus dwell time (see Appendix B). If the sub-grade ITC bus facility were full, the next bus arrival would have to go down through the facility, circulate past all the occupied bus berths, proceed back up to the street, circle around several blocks, and re-enter the ITC facility. It may be possible to stack some buses on the down ramp leading to the first bus berth or the bus only lane on Race Street.

2.3.3. Safety

As designed, the underground facility does not take into account the fact that buses will be fueled by compressed natural gas (CNG).[7] A high release rate gas leak from a bus in the facility could create an explosion hazard. CNG is stored aboard buses at up to 3,500 psi in cylinders located either on the roof or under the floor. Recent events at various locations where CNG is used indicate that a high percentage of fuel leak incidents occur when buses are parked after being operated, which is the type of operation that would occur in this facility. All possible methane accumulation locations and potential ignition sources must be identified and mitigated. Additionally, methane detection systems, proper forced ventilation and emergency notification and evacuation plans must be considered.

As the number of CNG fueled buses increases, there is a higher likelihood of a CNG-related incident occurring in the proposed underground bus facility. A prudent design must account for the operation of CNG fueled buses. The proposed design includes features that will make it difficult, at best, to incorporate recommended design provisions to mitigate the fire and explosion risk associated with CNG fueled buses. When handled properly and in a facility that is designed appropriately, CNG presents no greater risk than diesel fueled buses. However, improper handling or design can result in serious situations arising. Some design considerations recommended to make the facility CNG friendly are:

---

[7] Although nearly all road coaches are now diesel fueled, that is changing. One out of four transit buses built today is CNG fueled, and as emissions standards are tightened, a significant percentage of road coaches will be CNG fueled, also. Liquefied Natural Gas (LNG) will not be widely used, so is not included in this report.

- Beam – Ceiling Design:

Possibly the most restrictive design feature of the proposed underground facility is the use of tall profile concrete ceiling/floor beams. This type of design provides numerous pockets where methane, which is lighter than air, can accumulate. In the event of a high release rate leak from a bus parked in this facility, methane (CNG is 82-97% methane) will rapidly accumulate in these overhead pockets. An ignition possibility occurs within the flammability limits of 5-15% volume of CNG in air. In order to minimize the potential of methane concentrating up to the point where it falls within the lower and upper flammability limits, the beams, trusses and purlins should be an "open" design to prevent accumulation of methane. Alternatively, airtight ceiling panels could be used to close the pockets, although this option would significantly increase the cost of methane detection equipment required and significantly complicate the forced ventilation routing.

- Methane Detection:

Methane detectors should be located in all areas where it is likely that methane gas can accumulate as a result of either a high or low release rate leak from a CNG fueled bus parked in the facility. The design proposed for Option 2 would require numerous detectors. Detectors should be considered which will automatically initiate appropriate responses if methane is detected at 20% of the lower flammability limit (1% volume in air) at any location in the facility.

- Forced Ventilation:

In the event of a detection (see above), exhaust fans should be automatically operated, in conjunction with vents, louvers, etc., to provide adequate ventilation to effectively eliminate pockets of methane that can reach the lower flammability limit. The proposed design includes forced ventilation, but does not address stagnant pockets. Additionally, all fans, blowers and other equipment should be National Electric Code Class 1, Division 2 certified, since they will be operating in a gas rich environment in the event of a leak.

- Electrical Equipment:

All spark-generating equipment should be de-energized in the event of a leak. All electrical equipment in the travel path of the gas-rich air should be investigated and appropriate measures taken to eliminate, relocate or replace it with appropriate equipment. The National Fire Protection Association's NFPA 52 and applicable parts of NFPA 70 should be adhered to.

- Emergency Systems:

Detection of methane should, in addition to energizing ventilation, automatically sound appropriate audible alarms; display visual alarms and summon necessary personnel at the facility and from appropriate emergency response agencies, such as police and fire.

The central area for passenger loading and marshalling includes a combination escalator and central stairways, and an elevator for access between the upper and lower levels of the facility. This may be adequate for ambulatory patrons (redundancy of escalator and stairways), but may be inadequate for a sizeable expected population of patrons using mobility-aids (which is probable given that this is a tourist site). A bank of elevators may be necessary, and it is not clear whether the design can be modified to include the extra core space needed for a bank of elevators.

The evacuation of patrons in mobility-aids from the underground bus facility is problematic if the only exit route uses the relatively long, 6% grade up-ramps.

Buses starting to enter the underground ITC facility may have to back out onto Race Street when all bus berths are occupied. This may be the case even if some buses are allowed to stack on the down ramp to queue for the next available bus berth.[8]

2.3.4. Passenger Quality of Service

When all bus berths are occupied, the necessity for the next bus that arrives to proceed down and through the ITC facility, only to exit the facility and circle the block may be perceived by passengers on-board the bus as a frustrating, tedious waste of time. Many of these passengers will have traveled on their bus as much as 6 or 7 hours, and wish to dock for unloading as quickly as possible, without additional routing diversions. It may be possible to mitigate this possibility by providing a variable message sign (VMS), with sufficient advanced warning, to buses arriving on Race Street that would indicate that all bus berths within the ITC facility are full. Arriving buses would then proceed to circle the block and attempt to re-enter the ITC facility, depending on what status is displayed on the VMS as the bus initiates a second entry into the facility. This would at least avoid an unnecessary path through the ITC facility when all bus berths are occupied.

The central platform for passenger marshalling, and unloading/loading is not heated or cooled. During adverse weather conditions, this may pose a problem for the bus patrons.

As mentioned under safety considerations, an insufficient number of elevators are provided. This implies long wait times, even with a quick cycling of the elevator, for the elderly, and for persons with mobility-impairments who must use the elevator.

Park access would be convenient and safe to and from the sub-grade bus facility, although a single elevator, as proposed in the current design, would be inadequate to accommodate passenger volumes. In terms of comfort and ambience, the garage would be preferable to the surface lot options under a variety of undesirable weather conditions, although many passengers are likely to prefer the surface options in good weather, particularly if temperatures within the garage are not maintained at comfortable levels.

---

[8] Although nearly all road coaches are now diesel fueled, that is changing. One out of four transit buses built today is CNG fueled, and as emissions standards are tightened, a significant percentage of road coaches will be CNG fueled, also. Liquefied Natural Gas (LNG) will not be widely used, so is not included in this report.

When the bus bays are fully occupied, arriving buses may need to circulate through the garage, resulting in significant delay and inconvenience for bus passengers.

2.3.5. Operational Complexity

The design fails to consider the critical contingency of a disabled bus in one of the saw tooth bays that would require towing. A 45 foot tour bus requires a large, heavy-duty tow truck (approximately 30 ft. in length)[9]. The design proposes 16 bays around a central passenger loading and marshalling area, with buses circulating on the outside perimeter aisle. As many as three (3) turns are necessary to access a bus bay. There would be insufficient width in the aisle for a large tow truck to maneuver and establish a hookup with the disabled bus. In like fashion, turning radii are inadequate to permit a combination bus-in-tow to maneuver the curves (required turning radii are approximately 46 ft.)[10]. It is also not clear that vertical clearance, particularly on the ramps, is adequate. The relatively steep 6% upgrade on the ramps may pose negotiability problems with the extra load.

The only way to get the disabled bus out of the facility is literally to send in a crew to dismantle it, piece by piece, and crate it out. While this contingency is a very rare event, it could nevertheless pose a public relations problem for both the NCC and the NPS should it ever occur. There are approximately 25,000 bus arrivals per year at the INHP. This translates into 50,000 stopping events (drop-off/pick-up). Assuming a 50-year facility life, this translates into 2,500,000 stops at the bus bays. It is conceivable that at least once such an event will occur. The problem is that like the proverbial "100 year flood", it could happen tomorrow or 50 years from now.

Elaborate control procedures are necessary to make Option 2 work since no provision was provided for overflow slots. Controllers at the entrance to the facility need to have real-time occupancy status of each of the 16 berths in order to manage any stacking of buses on the down ramp.

To the extent that advanced scheduling and reservation of bus berths is a part of the operational control plan for this option (as well as Option 1), there are additional problems. The process is difficult to enforce, and there are always unexpected bus arrivals. Variance and unpredictability of bus ETA contribute to bus queuing in the access lane, and/or the occurrence of gaps in time during which the berth is not utilized in either drop-off or pick-up mode. In addition, not all slot times can be filled with advanced reservations. These problems also contribute to low capacity utilization. This in turn leads to a greater frequency of overflows.

2.3.6. Impact on Pedestrians

Buses are loaded and unloaded underground and do not interfere with pedestrian movement on the adjacent sidewalks to the INHP. Bus patrons as pedestrians are brought directly within one of the major destination attractions within the INHP.

---

[9] Data provided by Miller Industries, Inc., maker of heavy-duty tow trucks for commercial vehicles.
[10] Data provided by Miller Industries, Inc., maker of heavy-duty tow trucks for commercial vehicles.

An insufficient number of elevators between the underground loading/unloading platform and the upper levels of the NCC will increase the wait times for bus patrons with mobility impairments.

All pedestrian movements to the underground facility for bus loading and unloading are concentrated at the combined escalator/stairway/elevator core space and may result in some congestion during peak times.

2.3.7. Visitor and Environmental Impacts

This option may be considered to have the most favorable visitor and environmental impact, because the visual and auditory impacts of the buses would be hidden and the design would have the least intrusive effects on the park and museum.

Bus circulation on local streets is likely to be more intrusive than in other options, however, because access to Interstate 676 would require vehicles exiting the garage to proceed east on Race Street, south on 4th Street, east on Arch Street, and then north on 5th Street to the highway entrance. The location of overflow loading/unloading areas would present similar issues to the other options, although routing is likely to differ in that buses would most likely proceed from Race Street to 4th Street and Arch or Market Streets, before turning onto 5th or 6th Streets.

2.4. Option 3A

2.4.1. Overview

Option 3A is one of 3 options that both provide the recommended capacity of 16 berths and allow the ideal model concept of a single drop-off/pick-up location. The other two are the comparable Option 3B, and the much more costly Sub-Grade ITC, Option 2. Figure 2.4.1 shows Option 3A and the arrangement of the 16 berths located at the NCC building.

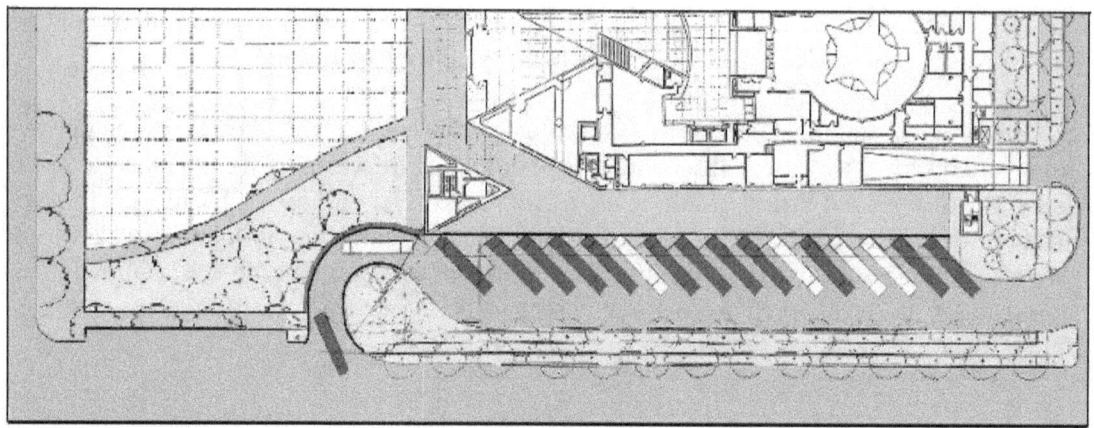

Figure 2.4.1. Option 3A - Saw Tooth Arrangement of 16 Berths

Buses are guided off Race St. by a controller into the bus aisle where they can pull into the first available berth. After loading/unloading passengers, buses would then travel out of the ITC onto 5th St., which offers the option of continuing through the 5th Street tunnel, turning right onto Race St., or entering the bridge ramp. In the rare instance when all 16 berths are occupied, arriving buses can be "waved off" by the entrance controller, and directed to either proceed to the overflow spaces or go around in a designated route and re-enter the ITC.

2.4.2. Capacity

The 16 berths of this option will satisfactorily meet demand 96% of the time under current peak bus arrivals as measured by ORA, assuming a 10-minute dwell time. It is quite possible that 16 berths in this arrangement will meet all current bus arrivals, in that and prudent management of the ITC can flatten the peak demand curve through advance scheduling and effective marketing. Overflow times are now projected to occur between 10: 00 – 11:00 A.M. and 12:00 – 1:30 P.M. on spring weekdays. To handle this overflow, it is proposed that 5 overflow spaces be constructed on the west side of 6th Street, with 3 spaces located opposite Block 3 and 2 spaces located opposite Block 1. These overflow spaces are designed as bus turnouts that do not require parallel parking maneuvers, but provide entrance and exit tapers to allow buses to leave and re-enter through traffic with a minimum disruption (see Chapter 3 for a detailed description).

2.4.3. Safety

Option 3A allows the highest level of passenger safety compared to the other options. Visitors to the Park are dropped off and picked up at a single location and can access the Park without crossing any streets containing through traffic. Passengers are also not required to cross any bus traffic in the ITC area. The saw tooth arrangement safely and efficiently segregates pedestrians from vehicle movements. This option also provides a protected marshalling area for passengers to gather after exiting and before entering their buses.

2.4.4. Passenger Quality of Service

By allowing a single drop-off/pick-up zone, Option 3A allows the maximum level of service to passengers and minimizes operational complexity of the system. By unloading next to the NCC building, it will be obvious to visitors which direction to start walking once off the bus. This option also allows safer Greeter locations at the facility.

Compared to Option 1, this option would eliminate the inconvenience and safety problems associated with use of the DRPA Bridge Triangle across Race Street. Access to the park and museum would be convenient, with the circulation of bus vehicles separated from the flow of pedestrians boarding and exiting buses.

On spring weekday afternoons under current demand, the 16 berths of Option 3A will handle 96% of bus arrivals. Since most of the bus arrivals at that time are for pick up the bus driver would circle around if there were no available berths. Those buses dropping-off passengers during that period (less than one per hour) will be routed to the overflow spaces on 6th Street. These passengers will then have to cross 6th Street in the process to get to the NCC, Visitor Center or Independence Hall

2.4.5. Operational Complexity

Option 3A allows the least complex operation of all of the options described in this report. All buses would enter the ITC from Race Street, where they would be guided to the first available berth (using the FCFS system). Greeters would meet arriving buses and obtain information from the drivers, which would be entered into the database. The buses would be given an identification number for display in the windshield, and then be directed to the long-term parking facility.

Upon returning to pick up passengers, buses again are guided into the first available berth by a controller, who enters the bus number and berth assignment into the database. The annunciation system then would announce the bus arrival and instruct passengers to immediately board.

During overflow conditions, buses would be directed to the overflow spaces, or instructed to circle and re-enter the ITC via an approved route.

2.4.6. Impact on Pedestrians

Only pedestrians on Race and 5th Streets will be affected by Option 3A. Pedestrians will have to cross the bus exit ramp when walking along 5th Street and the bus entrance driveway on Race Street. Both of these locations are proposed to be staffed with controllers, who can help with crossing pedestrians as needed. Under peak existing conditions, buses will enter and leave the ITC every minute or so, on average, so pedestrian conflicts are expected to be minimal.

2.4.7. Visitor and Environmental Impacts

This option would eliminate the disadvantages associated with use of the DRPA Bridge Triangle across Race Street (Option 1 and Option 4). Specifically, the additional circulation on local streets by buses first seeking space in the primary lot before being diverted to the DRPA Bridge Triangle is avoided. The consolidation of bus operations on Race Street and along only a small section of 5th Street at the intersection of Race Street should have a beneficial impact on the views and air quality at the park and its immediate vicinity. The greater effective capacity of Option 3A should reduce the frequency of overflow bus operations compared to other options, thus reducing any perceived negative impacts of overflow bus operations on the pedestrian environment and neighboring land uses.

An adverse impact of Option 3A would be the encroachment into the landscaped area in the southwest corner of the NCC site, resulting from the expansion of the bus facility footprint. The bus turnout to 5th Street would be visible from the terrace and park areas, whereas in other options the bus facility would be shielded from view by the NCC structure. This can be mitigated through construction of a "designer" wall structure that would effectively provide separation.

2.5. Option 3B

2.5.1. Overview

Following a review of Options 1 and 2, the Volpe Center review team decided that it could be possible to locate 16 berths at the NCC location without using the DRPA Bridge Triangle. This option consists of 11 saw tooth spaces located at the NCC building, 2 spaces on Race Street and 3 "overflow" spaces located on the eastern side of the ITC lot. The three "overflow" spaces are northbound parking, with access to them provided by continuing the radius turn at the ITC exit ramp at the south end of the bus aisle. The two spaces on Race Street could be reserved for buses with a known ADA requirement.

Following the presentation of the Volpe Center preliminary findings on 1/13/00, the City of Philadelphia indicated that it would be willing to consider allowing the ITC to consume an additional twelve (12) feet of the western side of 5th Street. Figure 2.5.1 shows this arrangement.

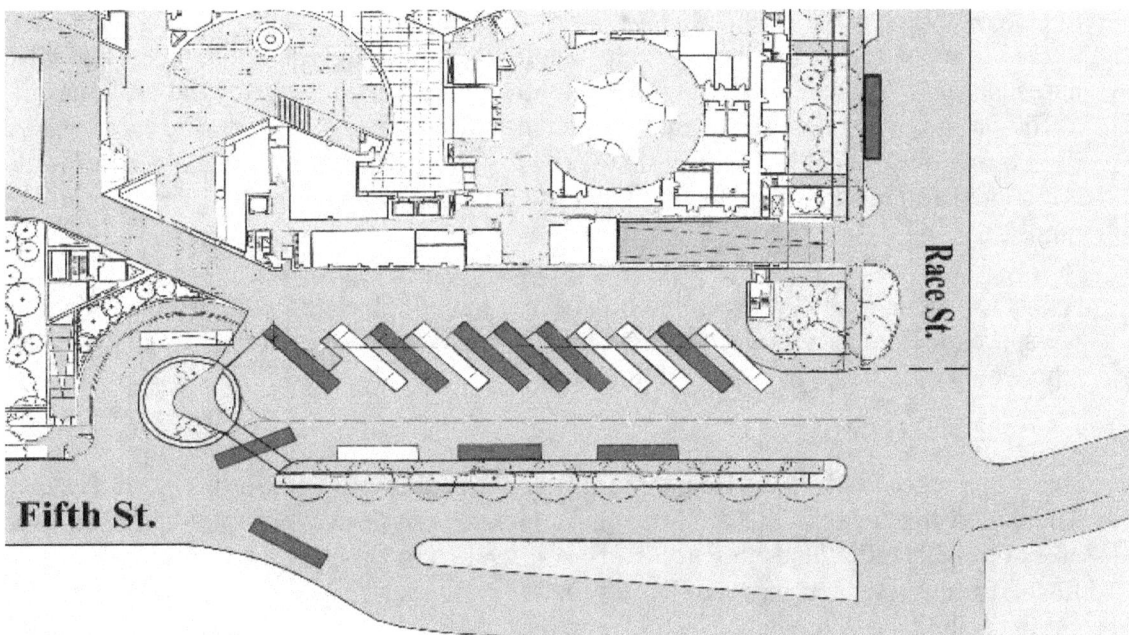

Figure 2.5.1. Option 3B Saw Tooth and Parallel Berths

The three berths on the east side of the lot are quasi-overflow berths, in that it is believed that they will be used almost exclusively for pick up only. Since actual dwell times for drop off will be significantly shorter than for pick up (e.g. 8 minute dwell time), the 13 berths, eleven alongside NCC and two on Race Street, will handle most drop offs under current demand, except during morning peaks on spring weekdays (10-11:00 A.M.).

These sixteen berths are proposed to operate on a First Come First Served (FCFS) regimen, described in detail in a subsequent section. For this reason, they will function as

16 berths, and will be sufficient for all but 4% of the time under current conditions. The overflow facility is recommended to be at the two locations on 6th Street as described in Option 3A.

2.5.2. Capacity

Assuming a 10-minute average dwell time[11] for loading and unloading passengers, the 16 berths of Option 3B do not see overflow conditions until more than 60 buses per hour is encountered. Per the ORA traffic and bus studies, this occurs only during spring weekdays between 12:00 – 1:30 P.M., when 64 buses per hour were counted. This means that 12 buses would be directed to the 6th Street overflow turnouts under worst case conditions today. Assuming that the afternoon peak can be softened through prudent management, including taking steps to minimize dwell times and outreaching to school and tour groups to schedule arrivals to flatten the peak arrival rates and spread them out throughout the day, it can be said that Option 3b will be adequate for all current bus traffic without utilizing any overflow spaces.

The Philadelphia Streets Department has expressed concerns with northbound buses exiting the 3 overflow berths of the ITC facility onto Race Street. Of particular concern to them is the perceived requirement for a third phase to be included in the 5th and Race intersection control, which they are reluctant to do. They suggested that the design have buses exit onto 5th Street just south of Race Street. This is a less then ideal design as the traffic on the two lanes west of the tunnel can only turn right. This traffic faced with a right arrow only signal will expect that it has exclusive right of way. This traffic would not anticipate potential conflicts with right turning traffic from the one lane east of the tunnel.

A Bus Controller will have to monitor activity at the two Race Street berths to ensure that the spaces are properly utilized. This function could also be performed by the Greeters who would meet buses at this location.

2.5.3. Safety

Buses can enter Race Street from either the 6th Street highway exit or the 8th Street exit. The first available berth on Race Street is far enough east from 6th Street to allow buses to cross through traffic lanes to enter it. Buses, which use this berth, can then exit it onto Race Street, as it is designed as a bus turnout of minimum 175-foot length, with a tapered entrance and exit, analogous to a highway on- or off-ramp. If a second berth is located here, the overall length would not be doubled, as the dedicated lane adjacent to the berth is for buses only, and allows reduced speed operation.

The buses that use one of the 11 saw tooth berths will exit the ITC lot onto 5th Street, in the same manner as the other options. The few buses that utilize the 3 quasi-overflow berths in the ITC lot will exit the lot onto Race Street. It is recommended that the

---

[11] 10 minutes is probably high for unloading operations and possibly low for loading operations, but it provides a good starting point for comparison of the different options. A primary focus in the future, regardless of the Option selected, should be for the ITC management and staff to work closely with bus groups to minimize all dwell times.

existing traffic stop line be moved westerly on Race Street to the western edge of the ITC entrance. To safely exit buses, the signal at 5th and Race can be modified to include a delay between 5th Street red and Race Street green to allow exit of the buses. Remembering that there will be perhaps 48 buses total exiting this way during non-peak through traffic times on Race Street, either the bus controller stationed at the ITC entrance/exit or a hired police officer could assist the buses to safely exit onto Race Street. This translates to an average of nearly 2 minutes between buses exiting onto Race Street under worst-case existing conditions, so a third phase is not needed in the Race and 5th Street controller.

Overall site safety is enhanced by the fact that the 16 berths could handle all existing bus traffic (assuming peak softening) and not using any on-street overflow berths as is true for Options 3A, 3C, and 4. The overflow spaces on 6th Street, then, would be able to accommodate growth. By designing these spaces as bus turnouts, buses will not have to parallel park to use them. The 6th Street design also affords traffic calming and increased pedestrian safety without diminishing the current level of service B[12]. There are currently levels of service E and F for some movements in the 5th Street area proposed for the overflow sight between Market and Arch Streets, so this option improves safety relative to the 5th Street overflow location.

Under Option 3B, there is the potential for conflicting bus movements in the central aisle when a bus is backing out of the western saw tooth berths simultaneous with a bus exiting the facility from one of the three quasi-overflow berths. For completely independent bus operations on both sides of the ITC there needs to be 36 feet in the central aisle. With the current design, there is only 27 feet. The bus controller would therefore need to hold the buses backing out of the saw tooth berths when one of the three eastern berth buses were to exit the facility.

This option would also require moving the stop line on Race Street back to the eastern edge of the ITC which would have a negative effect on the NCC garage exit. The garage entry/exit is too close to the existing stop line and could be blocked by queues of cars in any case (under all the Options). Signage, with some enforcement, may be necessary to warn motorists not to proceed forward if they will block the entry/exit to the garage.

There is a section of 12.75% grade per the architect's newest drawing at the return entrance into the south end of the ITC lot. Based on the configuration and bus dimensions, this grade presents a potential problem for buses returning into the lot when all saw tooth berths are full. Further analysis by Pennoni Associates, transportation engineers contracted by Pei Cobb Freed & Partners, shows that buses would have to depart on 6.2 percent downgrade and immediately enter on a 12.75 percent upgrade potentially creating a "roller coaster effect."

The Volpe Center made a scaled template of the design vehicle ("typical" 45 foot tour bus) and conducted simulated movements of a bus negotiating the ramp with the vertical road profile as indicated by the PCF drawings. While it is tight with respect to the

---

[12] See 6.9, Appendix E, Level of Service Definitions for more detail

approach, break over and departure angles of the vehicle, the bus can negotiate the ramp. For this reason, the Volpe Center recommends mitigation of the re-entry grade by use of a small embankment wall to separate the northern entry to the turnaround from the southern entry. Additionally, a guideline marking on the re-entry ramp to encourage buses to make the approach on a skewed angle will also effectively lower the re-entry grade. If both mitigation elements are in place, buses should not have a problem in negotiating the ramp.

There would have to be pedestrian fences installed along the island separating ITC adjacent to the NCC from 5th Street. These would prevent inadvert slipping into 5th Street into oncoming traffic.

2.5.4. Passenger Quality of Service

The FCFS regimen will minimize time that is spent on buses waiting for a berth to become available. All 16 berths are located at the NCC facility, so passengers will not be required to be picked up in a different location from where they were dropped off. It is proposed that Greeters take information from the bus drivers as passengers are unloading, which will reduce dwell times and improve overall operations. Passengers boarding buses in the 4 quasi-overflow spaces will be protected by a canopy.

This option differs from 3A only in that the location of several bus berths on the east side of the parking lot, across from the 11 saw tooth berths on the west side, would require passengers to cross the parking lot, where buses will be in motion pulling into and out of the 11 berths. This is a disadvantage in terms of passenger convenience and safety, although it is not as serious as the problems associated with use of the triangular lot in Option 1.

2.5.5. Operational Complexity

While not as simple as Option 3A, the operation of Option 3B is relatively straightforward. At the heart of this operational scheme is the FCFS regimen, which is favored by bus drivers, as it is perceived as the most fair to all. Drivers who visit the ITC often will try "to park as far south as possible in the ITC lot (to get their groups closer to the door). Orth-Rodgers has suggested that it is desirable operationally to have buses enter the furthest south open berth first. To assist drivers in locating berths they suggest putting electronic loops under each berth to record occupancy data that could be displayed at the entrance to the ITC indicating free berths.

Buses arriving to drop off passengers will pull into the first available of the 11 berths along NCC. Once they are full then a bus controller can signal to the next buses to take the 2 berths on Race Street. If the berths on Race Street are occupied (or reserved for a known ADA requirement) during peak days, then the bus will turn into the ITC lot and the bus will return into the lot via the turnout at the south end and take the forward most open space of the 3. There will be Controllers located at both ends of the ITC bus aisle to direct bus movements and offer assistance when needed.

In drop-off mode, buses will exit the ITC when all 16 berths are occupied and proceed via the designated routing to the overflow facility on 6th Street (described in Section 3.2.1.). Pick-ups are constrained to take place at the NCC only. In pick-up mode, drivers will have a choice of two routings: (1) proceed around the block and reenter the southern end of the ITC to access the 3 quasi-overflow berths; (2) proceed via a designated routing that brings the bus back onto Race Street where all 16 bus berths are now accessible again (1 (or 2) on Race Street, 11 adjacent to the NCC, and the 3 quasi-overflow berths at the eastern edge of the ITC). The choice will be left to the driver, but all routings will be illustrated on a card that can be given to the driver.

Greeters will collect information from bus drivers as passengers are unloading, give the drivers placards with identification numbers and record this information into the system via hand-held data logging devices. These devices will also enable all employees to access the database and answer passenger questions about bus locations, etc. Bus drivers can instruct their passengers that they need to be at the NCC 10 minutes before scheduled departure.

When buses return to pick up their passengers, as soon as a Greeter or Controller knows which berth a bus will enter, this information will be added to the system, and the information displays will show the berth assignment. A public announcement system will broadcast this information, also. The placard numbers on the buses identifies those buses and tour groups in the system, but are transparent to the passengers. The Greeter will collect the placards as passengers are loading.

Since there is not enough room for independent backing maneuvers of opposite buses from the saw tooth berths and the three quasi-berths a Bus Controller would have to provide manual direction to minimize the potential conflicts.

2.5.6. Impact on Pedestrians

Pedestrians walking north on 5th Street will have to cross bus traffic exiting the ITC and also re-entering the lot during afternoon peaks, but the frequency of bus traffic under the worst existing conditions is 1 bus every minute or so. Option 3B affords ample pedestrian capability on 5th Street. The berth(s) on Race Street will require pedestrians on the south side of Race Street to negotiate through tour groups milling on the sidewalk there, but the sidewalk is more than ample to accommodate this. We recommend that the sidewalk be no less then 15 feet to accommodate bus passenger and pedestrian traffic. The number of pedestrians using this sidewalk is expected to be small in all the Options.

Since the 16 berths at the ITC will handle virtually all existing buses, and will probably be able to handle more with prudent management, pedestrians in the general NCC vicinity will encounter few problems with bus passengers to the NCC.

2.5.7. Visitor and Environmental Impacts

Visitor and land use impacts would be similar to those of Option 1, although the disadvantages associated with use of the triangular lot across Race Street would be eliminated and the frequency of overflow bus operations would be reduced, as in Option 3A. Unlike Option 3A, however, the bus facility would not be expanded into the landscaped area in the southwest section of the site and adverse visual impacts on the NCC and the Mall, therefore, would be reduced. Any adverse visual impact of the bus facility and operations would be modest and could be further mitigated with design and landscaping treatments.

2.6. Option 3C

2.6.1. Overview

This option includes 11 deep saw-toothed berths adjacent to the NCC, 2 berths on the southern edge of Race Street, 3 deep saw-toothed berths on the DRPA Triangle island, and overflow slots (assumed number is 7) on 5th Street. The access to and from the 3 berths on the triangular island, however, is radically changed from Option 1. These 3 bus berths are re-oriented towards the Ben Franklin Bridge entrance ramp at 5th Street, with access to them via a new driveway cut off this entrance ramp. Exit from these berths is via a new driveway cut onto Race Street. Figure 2.6.1 shows this option.

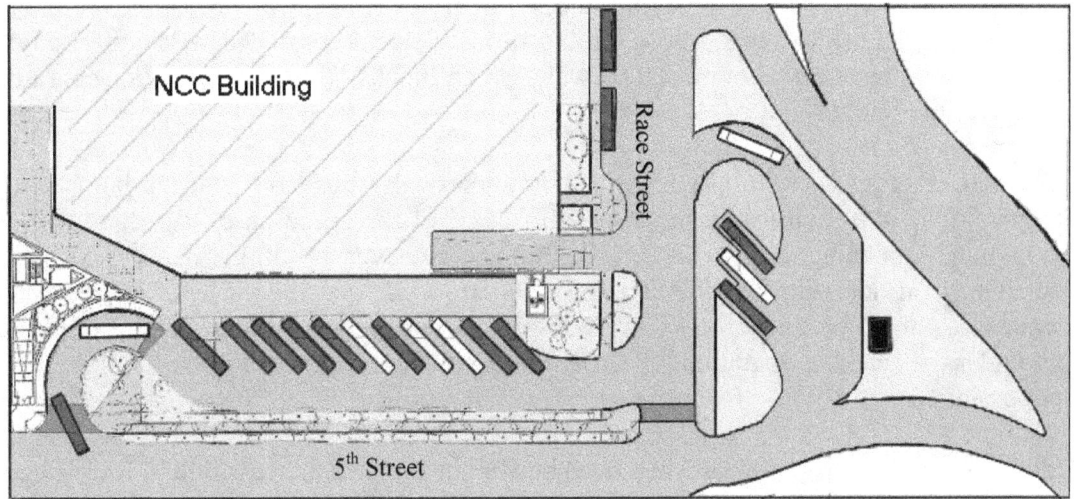

Figure 2.6.1. Option 3C – Saw Tooth and Race Street Berths

This option also proposes shortening the "go-around" routing for buses during pick ups when all 16 bus berths are occupied. The next bus arrival(s) would be routed north on 5th Street, through the triangular island on a pass-by, and back onto Race Street for re-entry into the primary component of the ITC adjacent to the NCC. The two berths on Race Street could be reserved for buses with a known ADA requirement.

It is proposed to use the simplified bus management and control system, with the FCFS regimen, to tie together the three main components. These consist of the 16 bus berths in the primary bus facility (i.e., the 11 at the NCC, 2 on Race Street, and 3 on the northern edge of Race Street in the DRPA triangular island).

2.6.2. Capacity

Option 3C nominally has 16 bus berths in the primary bus facility consisting of the three components identified above. Each bus berth permits independent entry and exit, and would sustain an operation with no overflows 96% of the time under present bus arrival conditions during the peak, assuming average dwell times for buses at 10 minutes.

One problem with this option is that the 3 bus berths sited on the triangular island are likely to have substantially greater than 10-minute average dwell times, at least during pick-up mode. This is because passengers will have to walk an extra 200-250 ft to access bus berths #14, #15, and #16 on the triangular island. Passengers will also experience extra crossing delay at Race and 5th Street. This adds an extra 80 seconds to the average dwell time for pick-ups.[13] Therefore, the 3 berths within the DRPA triangular island are likely to have average dwell times on the order of 12-13 minutes, at least in pickup mode. This means that Option 3C, with its 16 bus berths, operates at less capacity than the preferred configuration of bus berths in Option 3A, for example.

Another concern with having buses exit the DRPA Bridge Triangle onto Race Street is that traffic stopped eastbound on Race Street will block the exit driveway. Buses that are waiting to exit will then be blocking access to these berths, with the spillover likely occurring on the bridge ramp. Buses trying to turn left into the DRPA Bridge Triangle berth area will have no recourse but to wait, which blocks the bridge ramp, or continue north over the bridge.

Option 3C also proposes to use 5th Street for additional 7 bus slots, stacked bumper-to-bumper. Our objection to the proposed utilization of the space on 5th Street for buses loading and unloading during overflow conditions, however, is still germane. The space constraints on locating bus berths opposite Block 2, between Market Street and Commerce Street, permit three (3) well-designed bus turnouts. Independent entry and exit under the stacking conditions (i.e., bumper-to bumper) proposed under Option 3C is not possible.

Option 3C proposes to utilize the two sited bus berths on the southern edge of Race Street after the 11 berths adjacent to the NCC are occupied. In other words, buses are instructed to proceed first to the 11 berths adjacent to the NCC. If these are all occupied, a Bus Controller on Race Street would flag an arriving bus into the Race Street berths directly.

2.6.3. Safety

There are two major safety concerns associated with use of the 3 bus berths on the DRPA triangular island. First, bus drivers using the triangular island as a pass-through on a "go-around" must exit onto Race Street, make a left-turn and simultaneously cross two (2) lanes of through-traffic to access the curbside lane for reentry into the ITC at the NCC. These maneuvers must be made over a very short distance of approximately 120 ft.

---

[13] Calculations based on an assumption of a pedestrian speed of 4 ft/ second, and a 30-second pedestrian phase within a 90-second cycle length (45 seconds each phase) for the signal at Race and Street. Fifth Street has a concurrent WALK interval 30 seconds long, 9 seconds flashing DON'T WALK (Race Street is 36'), 6 seconds yellow and red clearance. Pedestrian delay when arriving at any time during WALK is zero and the maximum delay when arriving at the beginning of the flashing DON'T WALK is 60 seconds. Therefore, pedestrians on average must wait 20 seconds per cycle to cross at Race and5thStreet. This also assumes that all pedestrians can cross within the first pedestrian phase. This may not be the case when the 3 berths are simultaneously loading, and as many as 120 passengers must cross. Sources: average pedestrian flow speed from Figure 4.2, Traffic Engineering Handbook, 1965 edition; cycle length at Race and 5thStreet from Orth-Rodgers & Associates, Inc., Traffic Data and Analysis: Final Report, p. 12.

Conflicting vehicular movements consisting of cars exiting the NCC underground garage and making a right turn onto Race Street further complicate this routing. An exiting car is in the blind spot of the maneuvering bus, and the differences in height of the two vehicles further adds to the difficulty of establishing a good sight-line.

Second, access to the 3 bus berths on the triangular island is via a new driveway cut off a major bridge/highway ramp. The Volpe Center is unaware of any other situation like this. Drivers' expectations are for a continuous flow on the bridge/highway ramp, and would be unprepared for a slowed vehicle making a left-turn into a driveway off the ramp. The situation is hazardous and could lead to a sizeable risk of rear-end collision. Furthermore, the driveway cut is only approximately 80 ft from the intersection of the bridge/highway ramp (the Ben Franklin Bridge) and Race Street, a major multi-lane urban arterial. Vehicles following a lead bus, at the end of a green phase at the intersection of Race and 5th Street, could easily spill back into the intersection when the lead bus slows to turn into the driveway to access these berths. Additionally, the 2 northbound lanes of traffic on Race Street merge into one lane on the ramp in the area where the proposed new driveway would be located. This exacerbates the issues associated with multiple use of the bridge ramp.

There are also safety concerns with pedestrians, particularly in drop-off mode, crossing at mid-block. It is recommended that a pedestrian fence be placed along Race Street in front of these three berths to channel the pedestrian flows to the crossing at Race and 5th Street to the island platform. Pedestrians would then flow along the island platform, cross the turnout at the crosswalks, and enter the NCC and IHP at that point. In addition to fencing, signing and other design features, the greeter stationed at the triangle should be involved in directing pedestrians toward the proper crossing. Nevertheless, even with these design and operational modification suggested for Option 3C, there would inevitably be off-loaded bus passengers who would attempt to share the exit driveway cut and cross Race Street, mid-block, at that location.

Option 3C, like Option 3A, has a simplified and safe one-way flow pattern at the primary ITC component adjacent to the NCC. Unlike Options 3B and Revised Option 4, there are no conflicting bus backing maneuvers.

2.6.4. Passenger Quality of Service

Passengers loading and off-loading from the Race Street berths and from the group of eleven (11) adjacent to the NCC would experience good accessibility and convenience to the Independence NHP in general, and the NCC as a prime attraction in particular. Passengers dropped off or picked up at the 3 bus berths within the DRPA triangular island, however, will have substantially more inconvenient and inaccessible travel paths. They will experience longer walking distances and longer delays, particularly in the crossing of Race Street and 5th.

Passengers who choose to circumvent the preferred or desired pedestrian path by crossing at mid-block will have a more hazardous crossing. Even with a proposed canopy for the

41

3 berths on the triangular island, these passengers will be more exposed to inclement weather.

During overflow conditions when all bus berths are occupied, passengers on board buses waiting to off-load would experience some additional delay as the bus is diverted to an overflow facility or else issued a "go-around" routing to attempt a second entry into the facility. This is the same situation, however, as under Option 3A, 3B, and Option 4 (Revised). Passengers would experience substantial delays and inconvenience under a catastrophic failure for Option 3C (see Section 2.6.5).

As with Option 3B and Revised Option 4, this option adheres to the architectural/building line/view corridor constraint, permitting views through the park to the other historic sites, and not impacting passengers waiting within the park to board buses.

Provided the sidewalk is of sufficient width on Race Street, there should be no adverse impact to circulating pedestrians from passengers off-loaded or loading at the proposed bus berths on the southern edge of Race Street. Passengers loaded and off-loaded from the buses would have safe and convenient pedestrian paths to/from the Race Street berths and the group of eleven (11) berths adjacent to the NCC. Passengers using the triangular island bus berths would have longer, more circuitous pedestrian paths. Unless channeled along desired path lines, their paths and crossing would be more hazardous.

There would have to be pedestrian fences installed along the front of the 3 bus berths in the triangular island, and along the island separating the ITC adjacent to the NCC from 5th Street. These would prevent inadvertent slipping onto Race Street and 5th Street into oncoming traffic.

The northern edge of Race Street has little pedestrian traffic. Therefore, passengers loading and offloading at the triangular island berths are unlikely to have any impact on circulating pedestrians. In any case, there is a width of approximately 20 ft., more than sufficient to handle both without any interference.

2.6.5. Operational Complexity

Unlike Options 3A, 3B, and Revised Option 4, Option 3C fails to adhere to a fundamental concept. The ITC facility needs to be segregated or insulated from the surrounding traffic so that bus operations, with entry and exit to/from the bus berths, and bus circulation through the facility do not interfere with the surrounding traffic. Conversely, the surrounding traffic must not interfere with the operational performance of the ITC. Bus-to-vehicle interference needs to be reduced to a minimum; in effect, the design of the ITC must de-couple the performance of each system to the maximum extent possible, which is not the case for Option 3C.

Option 3C requires buses to interact with the surrounding traffic in several, unintended ways. First, as discussed under Safety, slow buses turning left into the triangular island can lead to queues of following vehicles spilling back across the intersection of the bridge/highway ramp with Race Street.

Secondly, the release of buses from the triangular island via the new driveway cut onto Race Street can lead to very serious problems. This is because buses under Option 3C are released at an uncontrolled, non-priority intersection (the intersection of the new driveway cut with Race Street). This is not the case under Option 3B. Under Option 3B, some buses are also released onto Race Street, but the buses can be released easily, safely, and without undue delay. This can be accomplished by extending the concurrent red phase of the signal at Race and 5th Street. Buses can be released under signal-controlled conditions, without any adverse impact on the traffic on Race or 5th Street. The physical closeness of the point of release of the buses from berths #13, #14, #15, and #16 under Option 3B, and a proposed distance offset for the stop lines at both Race and 5th Streets also aid in this endeavor. Only an additional 6 seconds is needed to effect the release of each bus. A bus can be released every half a cycle (approximately 45 seconds for a 90- second cycle), whenever there is a phase transition between the two streets.

There can be substantial delays to a bus at the driveway cut attempting to turn onto Race Street. If the bus had completed a pass-by only through the triangular lot, and needed to cross two (2) lanes of traffic on Race Street in order to re-enter the ITC, the delay to the bus is even more substantial. Table 2.6.1 illustrates the order of magnitude of required time for a single lane crossing.

Table 2.6.1. Bus Merge Delay (seconds) Upon Re-entering the Traffic
Stream from the Triangular Island Exit Driveway[14]

Traffic Flow Vehicle/Hour/Lane (VPHL)	Critical Gap Duration (τ) (seconds)		
	8	10	12
	Average Time Required for Critical Gap to Appear (seconds)		
100	4.8	6.2	7.8
400	8.3	12.4	17.8
700	14.2	24.2	39.6
1000	24.1	46.9	87.8

Note: Bus merge delay is based on application of Garwood's model, i.e., $D_{merge} = 1/\mu \exp(-\mu\tau) - \tau / (1-\exp(-\mu\tau))$, where $\mu = vphl/3600$ and $\tau = $ critical gap duration in seconds.

As an example, even with only moderate flows of 350 vphl, a bus which has just completed a "go-around" pass-by through the triangular lot and needs to cross the two lanes of through traffic on Race Street to re-enter the ITC could be stopped at the driveway exit for a delay of approximately 40 seconds. This assumes the bus requires a 12-second gap to safely undertake the crossing.

---

[14] Garwood derived an expression of delay to a pedestrian or to a vehicle searching for a gap of sufficient duration to proceed safely across a traffic stream consisting of random (Poisson) arrivals at the point of crossing. His derivation proceeded from an expression for the probability distribution of the longest interval in a line of unit length divided by n random points.

Analysis of the delay to a bus at the release point for Option 3C shows it can lead to a catastrophic failure of interlocking queues.[15] The following scenario indicates just one of several instances where interlocking queues could gridlock traffic in the NCC area. Occurrences which are necessary (and are probable with respect to their occurrence, given an inability to control variability in bus arrivals and departures) are:

1. bunched departures from the three berths on the triangular island;
2. an inability to release these departing buses quickly, for whatever reason and
3. bunched bus arrivals at the NCC when the 13 bus berths (2 on Race Street, 11 saw tooth at NCC) are occupied.

An example scenario is:
- Initial bus is stopped at the driveway exit for a time interval about a cycle length.
- During this same interval, there are bunched departures from two berths, #16 and #15 for example.
- During this same interval, a new arrival at the NCC is diverted north on 5th Street to the triangular island berths.
- The new arrival can not enter the triangular island. The restricted stacking space can only hold the two departing buses (which must wait for the initial bus to be released at the driveway exit). This is because of the tight physical space of approximately 90 ft. only, forcing the arriving bus to stop at the entrance driveway on the bridge/highway ramp.
- During this same interval, vehicles behind the arriving bus to the triangular island start to queue and spill beyond the intersection of the ramp with Race Street.
- During this same interval, there is now a phase transition to green for traffic on Race Street.
- This traffic, however, having queued for the green phase serving 5th Street, can not now be released because of the blocking queue from the ramp.
- During this same interval, traffic continues to queue on Race Street during its green phase, eventually blocking the driveway exit from the triangular lot.
- There now exists a series of interlocking queues. The queue blocking Race Street cannot dissipate due to the stopped bus on the ramp at the triangular island's entrance. This bus, in turn, is blocked by the stationary departing buses within the triangular lot. These two buses cannot be released because of the lead bus stalled at the exit from the triangular island. This lead bus is stalled because of the queue of vehicles on Race Street, which cannot be released because of the blocking queue from the bridge/highway ramp.
- If the queues continue to build, secondary effects include buses exiting at 8th Street and 6th Street unable to enter the ITC facility because they too become entangled in the traffic. Moreover, buses waiting to depart the primary bus facility adjacent to the NCC may be unable to do so because the queues on 5th Street now extend back and beyond the exit of the ITC facility onto 5th Street.

---

[15] P. Roberg, "The Development and Dispersal of Area-wide Traffic Jams," *Traffic Engineering & Control*, June 1994, pp. 379-384.
C. Wright and P. Roberg-Orenstrein, "Simple Models for Traffic Jams and Congestion Control," *Proceedings Instn Civil Engineers Transpotation.* August 1999, pp. 123-130

A controller, seeing the three bus berths unoccupied or very soon to be, and faced with the bunched new bus arrivals, will divert them to the triangular lot. It is very possible to have as many as 6 buses in a very confined space at the triangular island. Without quick release of the original 3 departing buses, it is possible to have 1 stopped within the driveway exit, 2 holding within the triangular island, and the 3 new bus arrivals stopped on the bridge/highway ramp, on the threshold of the driveway entrance. Since there is very little space for stacking any vehicles on the ramp (approximately 80 ft.), even the third new bus arrival can spill beyond the intersection of the ramp with Race Street. The traffic dynamics described above can (not necessarily will) start. Also, the 16 nominal berths now act more like 14 or 14+ with regard to capacity of the combined components of the ITC under Option 3C.

2.6.6. Impact on Pedestrians

Pedestrians walking north on 5th Street will have to cross bus traffic exiting the ITC lot during afternoon peaks, but the frequency of bus traffic under the worst existing conditions is 1 bus every minute or so. Option 3C affords ample pedestrian capability on 5th Street up to Race Street. However, passengers loading and unloading at the DRPA Bridge Triangle berths will impede through pedestrians at the intersection of 5th and Race Streets. This is, though, a small number of people. The berth(s) on Race Street will require pedestrians on the south side of Race Street to negotiate through tour groups milling on the sidewalk there, but the sidewalk is more than ample to accommodate this.

2.6.7. Visitor and Environmental Impacts

Visitor and land use impacts would be similar to those in Option 1, although the use of local streets, including 4th, Arch, and 7th, by buses diverted from the primary ITC lot to the triangular lot across Race Street would be eliminated. This option therefore is preferable to Option 1 in terms of land use and environmental impacts. As described earlier, however, utilization of the 3 spaces in the triangular lot would not be as efficient as the utilization of spaces in the primary lot. As a result, the incidence of overflow conditions would be higher than in Options 3A and 3B, and the minor nuisance effects on land uses adjacent to overflow bus berths (on 5th or 6th Streets) would occur somewhat more frequently.

Compared to Options 3A and 3B, Option 3C has the advantage of avoiding any expansion of the primary ITC lot as currently designed, either into the southwest section of the NCC site (Option 3A) or at the western edge by 5th Street (Option 3B).

2.7. Option 4

2.7.1. Overview

This Option is a revision to a design proposed by Pei Cobb and Freed which included a group of eleven (11) deep, saw-toothed bus berths adjacent to the NCC, joined by four (4) shallow, saw-toothed bus berths on the eastern edge of the ITC opposite a central access aisle. This original Pei Cobb Freed design included an expansion of the existing eastern curb eight feet (8') eastward into Fifth Street. The Volpe Center review found this original design seriously flawed due to safety considerations: operational and safety problems with conflicting, bus backing maneuvers undertaken in the presence of restricted sight lines. Our findings about the original design confirmed similar findings by the traffic and site-engineering consultants (Orth-Rodgers et. al.) about this option as initially proposed.

Following the presentation of the Volpe Center preliminary findings on 1/13/00, the design of this option was revised in several significant ways so as to address safety and operational concerns. Most importantly, the City of Philadelphia indicated its willingness to allow the ITC to expand an additional twenty six feet four inches (26'-4") from the existing curbline eastward into 5th Street (rather than the 8' of the initial proposal). Approval of the City Ordinance necessary to formalize this approved curbline relocation is expected by City Council in the summer of 2000. Option 4 was revised in accordance, from what was presented to the Volpe Center on 1/15/00; as revised and as illustrated in figure 2.7.1. below Option 4 consists of the following elements:

- 2 bus berths on the southern edge of Race Street between 6th Street and the entrance to the underground NCC parking garage (rather than the three of the original proposal);
- 11 deep, saw-toothed bus berths adjacent to the NCC, on the western edge of the ITC facility; and
- 3 shallow-toothed bus berths on the eastern edge of the ITC facility. As noted above, the eastern curbline of the island platform servicing the three shallow, saw-toothed bus berths has been shifted east from the line of the existing curbline by 26'-4".

Figure 2.7.1 shows the revised saw tooth berth arrangements for Option 4. The two Race Street berths in Option 4 as revised, not shown in the figure, are located between 6th Street and the entrance to the underground NCC parking facility.

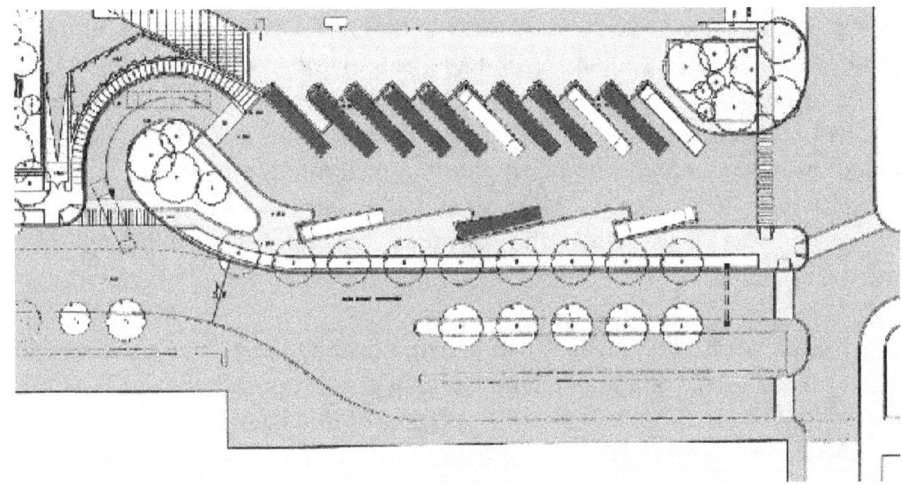

Figure 2.7.1. Option 4 (Revised) – Deep and Shallow Saw Tooth Berths

2.7.2. Capacity

The three bus berths proposed in the original Option 4 would have been sited on the southern edge of Race Street, occupying a block face length of approximately 185 feet. This would have resulted in a bus berth size of approximately 62 feet. Although the adjacent access lane is marked as "no thru traffic", in effect a "bus use only" lane, the resultant three bus berths would have been too small to permit independent entry and exit. The capacity of these three berths was therefore determined to be less than the nominal number.

Minimum and preferred design lengths for an on-street bus berth are L+25 meters and L+40 meters respectively. For a design vehicle equal to a 45-foot. tour bus, this translates to 127 and 175 feet. respectively. Because of the specific site conditions involving an adjacent access lane that prohibits thru traffic (in effect, a "bus only lane"), the minimum design length for a bus berth can be reduced. The revised schematic drawing (Drawing No. SKA-101C, 1/17/00) shows a potential change to the curb line at 6th Street and Race Street. The Volpe Center highly recommends that a minor design modification be made which would incorporate a curb extension as shown on the schematic. This would positively protect the adjacent "no thru traffic lane", converting it into an adjacent "bus only" access lane to the sited bus berths.

Based on these recommendations, Option 4 as revised now incorporates two (2) bus berths (rather than three), each approximately 90 ft. each, sited on the southern edge of Race Street. This revision permits independent entry and exit for each, in conjunction with the protected access lane adjacent to these two berths. Locating two (2) bus berths is workable and operational with the proposed design modification. The two berths could also be reserved for buses with a known ADA requirement.

Despite moving the island platform 26'- 4" eastward, with additional width added to the central aisle, the eleven (11) deep, saw-toothed bus berths and the three (3) shallow, saw-toothed bus berths operate as less than an equivalent number of berths (14) if sited to

47

provide complete independence of entry and exit. This is because the common aisle, at the resultant width of approximately 29 feet, is still too narrow to allow independent movement or to prevent encroachment by maneuvering buses. Assuming operation of a simplified bus management and control system involving a FCFS regimen, however, the three (3) shallow, saw-toothed bus berths on the eastern edge of the ITC facility should be used relatively infrequently. This would be during overflow conditions only (primarily, spring weekdays) when the "primary bus facility" consisting of the Race Street berths, and the eleven (11) berths adjacent to the NCC are all occupied.

Based on the scale of the PCF&P revised schematic drawing (Drawing No. SKA-101A, 1/17/00), it looks like the loading island serving the proposed three (3) shallow saw-toothed berths is 20 ft. In other words, with shifting of this island eastward, PCF allocated 10 additional ft. to the loading island, and 6 additional ft. to the central aisle.

The width of this island (assuming a concurrent loading of 160 passengers at 4 in-line parallel berths, as indicated in our original Option 3B) need only be approximately 14 or 15 feet.[16] With only three (3) berths now loading/unloading at this island, a proposed allocation of 15 feet for this island is even more pertinent (concurrent loading of only three buses, or 120 passengers total). The Volpe Center recommends that either the sidewalk next to the NCC be redesigned or additional footage from 5th Street be found so that the eastern passenger area is as close to fifteen feet as possible.

2.7.3. Safety

Safety would be enhanced for the Race Street berths by incorporating the design modification, which shifts the existing curb line northwards (establishment of a curb extension) to protect the adjacent bus access lane. Increasing the berth size by reducing the number of sited berths to two (2), instead of the three (3) in the initial proposal, enhances safe operations.

As mentioned above, the central aisle is still too narrow to permit complete independence of operations between the group of eleven (11) and the group of three (3) bus berths (approximately 39 feet in the central aisle is needed for complete independence). There could be conflicting backing maneuvers under the current or even proposed modified design. Some of these would occur with one or the other or both buses within the blind spot zone. Bus controllers would have to carefully control the operation.

This option establishes a one-way flow pattern through the facility, with release or exit of all vehicles onto 5th Street.

---

[16] Calculations are based on a general rule of thumb formula. 1.3 meters of sidewalk width for loading a bus, and 0.8 meters of additional sidewalk width for circulating pedestrians for a flow rate of 35 pedestrians per minute. This yields $1.3 + (0.8)(3.6) = 4.18$ meters (13.6 ft), assuming the first 40 passengers load at berth #16, and the other 120 passengers must flow past berth #16 to the other three berths; see G. Giannopoulos, Bus Planning and Operation in Urban Areas: A Practical Guide, 1989.

There could have been a danger that patrons off-loaded at the island would filter through the ITC facility to access the NCC. To prevent this, Option 4 specifically restricts loading and unloading at the three (3) shallow-toothed, bus berths to use of the front door of the docked bus only, with pedestrian fences along the bus berth where necessary to help channel the pedestrian flow and prevent unwanted crossing of the ITC facility. It also incorporates a pedestrian fence on the eastern edge of the island platform to prevent inadvertent falls or encroachments onto 5th Street.

2.7.4. Passenger Quality of Service

Passengers loading and off-loading from the Race Street berths and from the group of eleven (11) adjacent to the NCC would experience good accessibility and convenience to the INHP in general, and the NCC as a prime attraction in particular. During overflow conditions when the group of three (3) on the eastern edge of the ITC is used, passengers on the island platform would experience a slightly longer and more inconvenient walk. A canopy on the island would provide limited protection from the weather and help mitigate some of the inconvenience.

During overflow conditions when all bus berths are occupied, passengers on board buses waiting to off-load would experience some additional delay as the bus is diverted to an overflow facility (if provided) or else issued a "go-around" routing to attempt a second entry into the facility. This however would be much less burdensome and frustrating than under Option 2.

As with all the designs, with the exception of 3A, this option adheres to the architectural/building line/vista constraint, permitting views through the park to the other historic sites, and not affecting passengers waiting within the park to board buses.

Visitor experience would be approximately the same as in Option 3B. Pedestrian circulation between the buses parked on the 5th Street side of the parking lot and the NCC would cross the path of buses pulling into and out of berths.

2.7.5. Operational Complexity

If Option 4 now uses a simplified bus management and control system with a FCFS regimen, there should be few problems using berths on Race Street and the group of eleven (11) berths adjacent to the NCC.

Operational complexity arises when the bus controllers must manage conflicting movements in accessing both groups of bus berths concurrently. This should only happen, however, relatively infrequently during overflow conditions.

Option 4 as revised incorporates the necessary design modifications (e.g., pedestrian fences) to help channel and control passenger flows from the buses loading and off-loading at the island platform.

2.7.6. Impact on Pedestrians

Provided the sidewalk is of sufficient width on Race Street, there should be no adverse impact to circulating pedestrians from passengers off-loaded or loading at the proposed bus berths on the southern edge of Race Street.

The island platform, even with the Volpe Center-proposed revised width of fifteen (15) ft. (as opposed to a planned twenty (20) feet), still provides continuity with the contiguous sidewalks on 5th Street. Pedestrian flows along this segment of 5th Street, however, are understood to be minimal.

Passengers loaded and off-loaded from the buses would have safe and convenient pedestrian paths to/from the Race Street berths and the group of eleven (11) berths adjacent to the NCC. Passengers using the island platform would have longer, more circuitous pedestrian paths, because they will be channeled by the fences and guide rails included in Option 4 as revised along desired path lines so that they will not have top cross the ITC facility through standing and maneuvering buses.

2.7.7. Visitor and Environmental Impacts

Visitor and environmental impacts would be the same as in Options 3A and 3B.

3. Overflow Facility

As presented in Section 2.0, the preferred concept for an ITC consists of three elements: a "primary bus facility"; an overflow facility for drop-offs only; and a long-term parking facility for stacking buses before pick-ups. All three components need to be linked and to work as a system. The mechanism for making this happen is a simplified bus management and operational control plan, the general outline of which is delineated in Section 2.0.

3.1. Overflow Facility Logic

NPS must plan for overflows irrespective of a proper and judicious sizing of the primary bus facility. The Volpe Center has constructed a crude estimate of the magnitude of the overflow conditions under different values for the number of bus berths (see Appendix B). It is a crude measure of impact (MOI) of the aggregate affect of overflow conditions for the ITC during the spring weekday season, which is the peak period for visitor attendance at the INHP. It responds to the request of the NPS staff expressed during our discussions on 1/10/00.

Several conclusions are suggested by this analysis:

- Under current peak-load bus arrival conditions, 16 bus berths (total number in combined primary bus facility and overflow facility) seems to be a minimally sufficient number to reduce to a marginal impact the occurrence of overflow events.

- Under projected bus arrival conditions of 85 buses per hour at peak, this number (N=16) fails. To obtain near equivalent performance (i.e., minimal overflow events), the minimally sufficient number of bus berths is 21.

- Upgrading from N=14 bus berths to N=16 bus berths under current peak-load bus arrival conditions yields an enormous gain in performance of the system. Similarly, under projected peak-load bus arrival conditions, upgrading from N=16 berths to N=21 berths yields a large gain in the performance of the system.

If the projected peak season, bus arrival conditions do materialize, an overflow facility will still have to be planned, designed and sited. This assumes that the preferred design option chosen now is either Option 3b, or Option 4 with 16 bus berths on site at the NCC. The Volpe strongly recommends that planning, design, and determination of a preferred site location are completed now (including the necessary Memoranda Of Understanding and political commitments to implement the facility). This would allow the overflow facility to come on-line before serious deterioration in the performance of the primary bus facility.

In reality, the only sensible site location(s) for the overflow facility is along one or more of the perimeter roads to the INHP. Other locations further away from the INHP would be inaccessible and inconvenient to passengers dropped off at the overflow facility who are destined for destinations contained within the INHP.

A concept-design for an overflow bus facility is proposed that is well sited on 6th Street, and works well with the primary bus facility on Block 3 and with a simplified bus management and control system. The proposed site location for the overflow facility is well situated to the locating of the primary bus facility layout that consolidates all bus bays on the northeastern edge of Block 3, adjacent to the NCC structure. This is an important consideration since movements to/from all three components need to be optimized jointly to minimize excess time and distance. The proposed site location is also well situated to the INHP, and the destinations contained therein (an equally important consideration). The design also makes 6th Street, which abuts the INHP more "livable", pedestrian-friendly, and attractive as a gateway to the INHP from the western section of the City. The combined size of the primary bus facility and the overflow bus facility is 21 berths. According to the analysis, an ITC facility sized at 21 berths, given present and future demand, should have virtually no overflows (see Appendix B).

3.2. Concept Design for the Overflow Facility

An overflow bus facility, consisting of a group of three (3) in-line bus turnouts and a group of two (2) in-line bus turnouts, is proposed to be sited opposite Block 3 and Block 1 respectively, on the western edge of 6th Street. The block length opposite Block 3 is at least 184 meters long (600 ft.). This is sufficient to permit three in-line bus turnouts, capable of holding a 45' bus. The bus turnout will have appropriate taper lengths to allow independent entry and exit at an approach speed of 30 km/h (20 mph) (see Figure 3.2.1 illustrating the geometric design of the bus turnout). This corresponds to our preferred design recommendation for the size of an on-street bus berth of L+40 meters. Each bus turnout is approximately 54 meters in length (175'), with a clear zone allowance of 4.6 meters (15') between each turnout, and a clear zone allowance of 6.1 meters (20') at each corner to preserve corner sight lines.

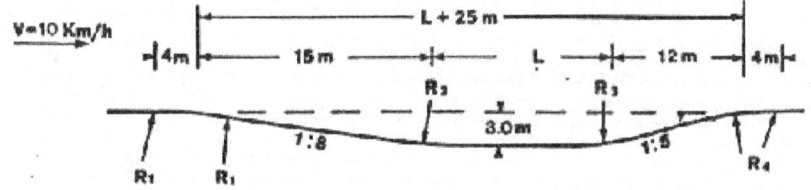

(A): Entrance with low speed, 10kms/hr. Radius of curb curves, R_1=20m, R_2=10m, R_3=10m, R_4=15m.

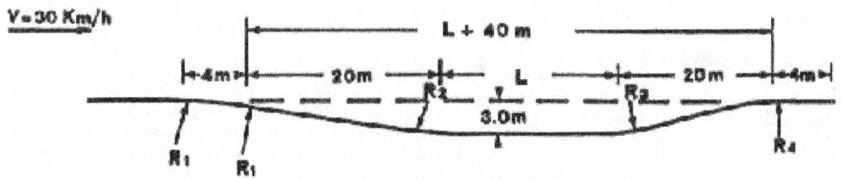

(B): Entrance at 30kms/hr. Radii of curb curves, R_1=40m, R_2=20m, R_3=20m, R_4=40m.

<u>Figure 3.2.1. Proper Bus Turnout Configurations</u>[17]

For the block opposite Block 1, the length to Ranstead Street, which splits the block, is approximately 92 meters (300 ft.). This is sufficient to permit two in-line bus turnouts, capable of holding a 45' bus. These turnouts will have appropriate taper lengths to allow independent entry and exit at an approach speed of 10 km/h (7 mph) (see Figure 1). This corresponds to our minimum design recommendation for an on-street bus berth of L+25 meters. Adequate clear zones would also be provided between each turnout, and at the two corners.

6th Street is an urban arterial, one-way southbound. The current cross-section includes 3 12' travel lanes and a 9' parking lane. For the segment in question (6th Street between Race and Chestnut, adjacent to the INHP), Average Daily Trips (ADT) is 9375 and weekday peak hour traffic flow on 6th Street is 894 vehicles per hour. Peak hour flow consists of right-turning movements onto Arch and through movements southbound on 6th Street at the intersection of *Arch and 6th*, which is the critical intersection for this road segment. The intersections at Market and 6th and at Chestnut and 6th have combined through and turning movement flows on 6th Street of 796 and 792 respectively. The relatively low ADT and peak hour traffic flows, the Volpe Center believes, allow a redesign of the cross-section of 6th Street between Race and Chestnut, permitting a reallocation of road space to pedestrian/bus patrons, buses, and bicycles, without any adverse affects on vehicular traffic flow.

A redesigned cross-section, assuming a minimum Right Of Way from building face to building face or lot line of at least 18.5 meters (60 ft.), would consist of a wide pedestrian sidewalk for circulation and bus drop-off of 3.7 meters (or greater) (12 ft.), a bus turnout width of 3.0 meters (10 ft.), an adjacent general purpose vehicular lane of 3.7 meters (12

---

[17] Source: G.A. Giannopoulos, <u>Bus Planning and Operation In Urban Areas</u>, 1989.

ft.), a second adjacent general purpose vehicular lane of 3.4 meters (11 ft.) combined with a 1.5 meter (5 ft.) bicycle lane for a curbside, left-sided[18] total lane width of 4.9 meters (16 ft.), and a combined planting strip and pedestrian sidewalk on the eastern edge of 6th Street (adjacent to INHP) of at least 3.0 meters (10 ft.).

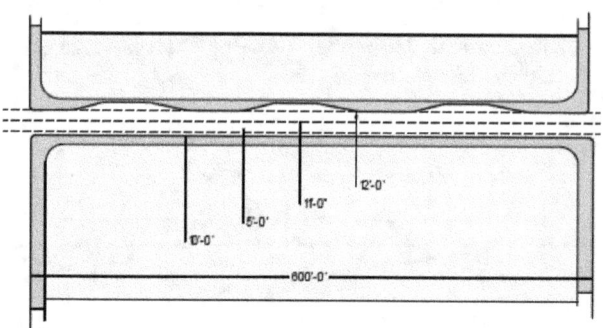

Figure 3.2.2. Overflow Locations on 6th Street

Pedestrians and bus passengers will be channeled to cross at Arch and 6th and Ranstead and 6th. This will be accomplished via two complementary approaches. At both crossings, two traffic calming devices consisting of the integration of a curb extension and a raised crosswalk will facilitate convenient and safe pedestrian crossings. Along the planting strip on the eastern edge of 6th Street, tree plantings combined with flowerbeds or dense shrubbery will gently dissuade mid-block crossings between the bus turnouts and the Independence NHP blocks. Alternatively, architecturally interesting and historically context-sensitive, cast-iron chain-linked bollards may serve that purpose[19]. The curb extensions will terminate the in-line bus turnouts, provide additional space for waiting pedestrians, enforce good corner sight lines, and shorten the time and distance exposure of pedestrians in the crossing. The raised crosswalk, which consists of raising the elevation of the crosswalk to the level of the adjoining sidewalk with up and down ramps for vehicular traffic, will make more visible and prominent the pedestrian crossing. It also will improve pedestrian to vehicle sight lines, slow approaching traffic, and facilitate easy movement of persons in mobility-aids. While the Arch and 6th Street crossing is signalized (the Ranstead and 6th Street crossing is not), pedestrians will inevitably cross at times against the light. The traffic-calming device consisting of a combined curb extension with raised crosswalk will make the crossing under these circumstances both safe and convenient[20].

---

[18] The wide outside lane is on the left side of the curb due to the one-way flow pattern southbound on 6th Street. Also, the bus turnouts must be on the right side or western edge of 6th Street because buses as yet do not have left-sided doors.

[19] One concept might be the use of bollards that reflect the old horse hitching posts used in Philadelphia at the time of the Revolutionary War.

[20] Since this is an important bus route, however, one has to be careful to select the right raised crosswalk profile and the right curb return radii on the corners. We want to traffic calm autos and pedestrianize the crossing but not affect speed and comfort too much for bus users, nor preclude right turns by long-wheelbase buses onto Arch; Source: E-Mail correspondence with Dr. Reid Ewing, P.E.

54

The final design component is a designated routing between the primary bus facility on the northeastern edge of Block 3 and the overflow facility. The designated routing is as follows: Buses unable to dock for drop-off at any of the bus bays on Block 3 would exit the primary facility, turn northbound on 5th Street, eastbound on Race Street, southbound on 4th Street, westbound on Arch Street, northbound on 7th Street, eastbound on Race Street, and southbound on 6th Street to the first or second group of bus turnouts in the overflow facility (see Figure 3.2.3).

3.2.1. Analysis of Concept Design

The preliminary analysis indicates the following for the critical intersection at Arch and 6th (at the terminus of the first group of bus turnouts). Given a two-phase cycle, cycle time of 60 seconds, and G/C ratio of 0.50, the capacity and corresponding saturation ratio for the current lane configuration, consisting of 3 12 ft lanes, are 2400 vehicles and 0.37 respectively. With the proposed two lane cross-section (1 12 ft lane and 1 11 ft. lane), capacity and saturation ratio are 1600 vehicles and 0.56. Total approach delay for the 3-lane configuration is 9.1 seconds per vehicle. For the proposed 2-lane configuration, total approach delay is 10.7 seconds per vehicle. The level of service (LOS) is B for the current lane configuration and for the proposed lane configuration, which does not change the existing condition. Mean queue length[21] per lane is 3.0 vehicles for the current 3-lane configuration. For the proposed 2-lane configuration, mean queue length per lane is 5.2 vehicles. There are no overflow queues[22] (failed cycles) for the current lane configuration and for the proposed lane configuration (see, also Appendix C).[23]

---

[21] Based on Little's equation, see W. Ashton, The Theory of Road Traffic Flow, 1966, p. 125.

[22] Based on Miller's equation, equation 8.82, see TRB SR165, Traffic Flow Theory, p. 161.

[23] The Volpe Center sent our concept-design and preliminary analysis for a quick peer-review to Dr. Reid Ewing, P.E. Dr. Ewing completed the two-year in the making state-of-the-art report on traffic calming for the Institute of Transportation Engineers (ITE), sponsored by FHWA. He is currently at work on a traffic calming manual for the state of Maryland, and is considered a nationally and internationally known expert on traffic calming, traditional neighborhood development (the New Urbanism), and the connection between transportation and land-use. With the usual caveat concerning a quick review only, Reid has consented to allow forwarding of his comments to US DOI/NPS, City of Philadelphia staff, and to the other stakeholders:

Without actually checking it, your capacity analysis looks right intuitively. Two through lanes should easily handle 900 vehicles per hour, particularly with one-way operation on both 6th and Arch. The one-way operation (two-phase signal) keeps your G/C ratio nice-and-high and presumably gives you a arrival type of 4 or possibly higher.

The reallocation of right-of-way is a great idea. It will make the street so much friendlier for pedestrians and transit users, without affecting motorists. There is no problem with the reduction of lane width to 11 feet, even with heavy bus use. It is an appropriate width, given the traffic calmed environment you wish to create. As for the combined curb extension and raised crosswalk, I like it in principle. Since this is an important bus route, however, you will have to be careful to select the right raised crosswalk profile and the right curb return radius on the corners. You want to traffic calm autos and "pedestrianize" the crossing but not affect speed and comfort too much for bus users, nor preclude right turns by long-wheelbase buses onto Arch. One small refinement: Why not consider a raised intersection rather than raised crosswalk? It is more costly but will calm traffic on both streets at once and pedestrianize the entire intersection.

The Volpe Center is aware of the political and value issues at stake in locating the overflow facility on 6th Street (or at a different location). These include routing concerns for buses diverted from the primary bus facility to the overflow facility, neighbors not wanting a bus drop-off in front of their property, and reluctance on the part of the City and other constituencies to redesigning the street. There are technical issues concerned with displaced parking for cars, and mitigation needed. There are also security concerns of parking buses, even temporarily, in front of abutting Federal buildings. These issues may be irresolvable.

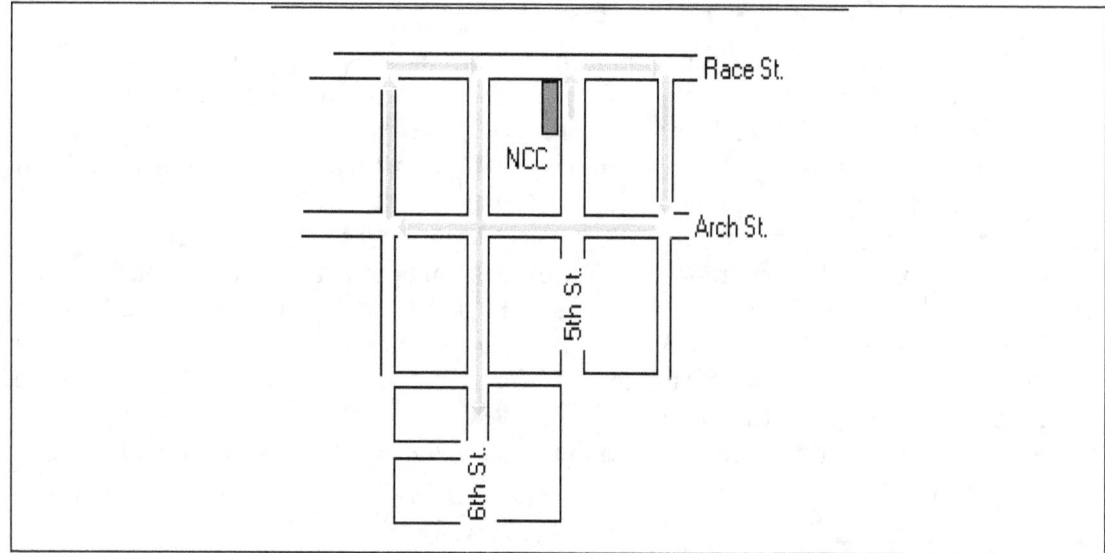

Figure 3.2.3. Designated Routing to Overflow Facility

However, the neighbors ought to be brought into this discussion and asked if they would prefer the current lane configuration (3 12 ft. lanes) which, based on the preliminary analysis, serves to increase speeds and is not necessary to accommodate volume, or a narrowed, traffic-calmed and "human-scaled" urban street with 1 12 ft and 1 11 ft. lane, and with slower speeds because of the raised crosswalks. Similarly, discussions with Federal agencies need to point out that use of the overflow facility would be controlled at all times, which may mitigate security concerns. Without both the primary bus facility and the overflow facility, the full potential of the INHP developments to serve as a catalyst for joint public and private investment in this area may not be realized. Locating the overflow facility on 6th Street does solve many problems (e.g., improved bus operations, no adverse impact on traffic, accessible, convenient and safer pedestrian crossings, enhanced quality and character of the INHP, reduction of traffic barrier effects which isolate the INHP from the urban fabric and associated developments). It may just be possible that a full airing of the proposed design and locating of the overflow facility on 6th Street will change some minds within NPS, City of Philadelphia, and PennDot staff.

The schematics (for potential future development) that Charles Newman, then Director of the City of Philadelphia's Capitol Program Office, provided to the Volpe Center show a proposed concept for a redesign of 6th Street, between Race and Chestnut, which would also narrow the street and include a bike lane on the western edge. Additional traffic calming devices, including curb extensions at Chestnut and 6th Street to slow approaching traffic are also illustrated on the drawings. Our concept-design, independently arrived at, simply flips the location of the bike lane to the eastern edge of 6th Street in order to accommodate the bus turnouts for the overflow facility on the western edge.

Narrowing the street in this way to permit locating of the overflow bus turnouts also connects both sides of the street for better pedestrian connectivity. This is important since there are sizeable flows (3-hour weekday evening period pedestrian flows are: 2236 at 6th and Chestnut; 2218 at 6th and Market; and 731 at 6th Street and Arch.[24]

Consider just the flows at 6th Street and Arch (which would be the crossing for the 3 bus turnouts). Without counting the additional pedestrian flows from the passengers off-loaded at the bus turnouts, narrowing the street width from its current 36 ft to the proposed 28 ft width (1 wide left curb-side lane consisting of a 5 ft. bike lane, and an 11 ft. general purpose vehicle lane, and an adjacent 12 ft general purpose vehicle lane) saves 2 seconds per passenger or 731* 2= 1462 seconds, using a generally accepted pedestrian speed of 4 ft/second[25]. The additional delay to vehicles at Arch and 6th Street from narrowing the cross-section is 1.5 seconds per vehicle or a *Total Approach Delay* increase of 894* 1.5 *1.05 (occupancy)=1408 seconds. Counting delays, its pretty much a wash, but the safety, convenience and amenity to pedestrians from a narrowed street is substantial, and this would apply to all crossings of 6th Street between Race and Chestnut.

It is also important to remember that the bus drop-offs opposite these buildings will occur relatively infrequently (1 bus an hour at current Spring time peak afternoons, up to 10-18 buses an hour at projected Spring peak afternoons). This is the case if the primary facility can be sized at 16 berths, which seems to be particularly critical for pick-ups because of the operational necessity of constraining all pick-ups to the primary bus facility site adjacent to the NCC (see Section 2.0). Baseline data also show an existing level of bus flows on 6th Street. It is not as if the abutting buildings are completely insulated from any bus activity.

The Volpe Center concerns with locating the overflow facility on 5th Street include:

- Constraining the overflow facility on 5th Street to opposite Block 2 only permits at best 3 independent entry/exit, well tapered L+25 meter bus berths (which for the 45 ft. tour bus as the design vehicle equals 127 ft). This is because Commerce Street splits the block; with the block face length between Commerce Street and Arch Street being approximately 400 ft., and the remainder of the block between Market and Commerce

---

[24] Orth-Rodgers, Traffic Data and Analysis: Final Report, p.15.

[25] Figure 4.2, Traffic Engineering Handbook, 1965 edition.

being approximately 130 ft. Our understanding is that the remainder of the block face cannot be used for an additional bus turnout. This is in contrast to locating the overflow facility on 6th Street where two groups of 3 and 2 (N=5) well-designed bus berths can be sited, with the former group of three bus turnouts at the preferred design length, with a higher approach speed.

- Because of the one-way flow patterns, 5th Street serves as a major connector to I-676 and I-95. This would make it difficult if not impossible to (a) narrow the cross-section of the road; and (b) install traffic calming devices such as curb extensions integrated with raised crosswalks to provide safe, convenient crossings for pedestrians and passengers off-loaded at the eastern edge of 5th Street. Again, this is not the case for 6th Street, where through traffic is coming off the interstates and the expectation of driving under various speed conditions is different as one enters a dense urban space. Therefore, pedestrian crossings can be channeled and made more safe, convenient and pleasant.

4. Capital and Operational Costs

4.1. Construction Cost Estimates

Design and development phase cost estimates for the Base Scheme (Option 1) and the Alternate Scheme (Option 2) were prepared for Pei Cobb Freed & Partners (PCF&P) by their cost estimation consultant, International Consultants, Inc. (ICI). No cost estimates were previously prepared for Option 3, which is proposed by the Volpe Center. A fourth option, which is a re-design of the original Option 4 that now includes an additional sixteen feet of 5th Street, was received by The Volpe Center after a meeting in Philadelphia on January 13, 2000. No cost estimates for this option have been prepared by the architect.

These cost estimates were reviewed and estimates for Option 3 and the new Option 4 were developed by the Volpe Center. The review and the developed estimates for Options 3 and 4 are elementary in nature, due to the limited amount of information available and the significant time constraints of the process. Table 4.1.1 shows a summary of the cost estimates for the base and alternate schemes as estimated by ICI. This is the cost information that was provided to the Volpe Center and formed the basis for the Volpe Center review.

Table 4.1.1 Cost Estimates for the Two Proposed Options[26]

Option	Date of Estimate	Total Estimated Cost
1. Base Scheme (Surface)	June 6, 1999	$10,349,977
2. Alternate (Underground)	September 7, 1999	$19,535,778
Additional Cost for Underground Bus Facility		**$9,185,800**
Additional Cost Without Level 3 Parking		**$8,579,813[27]**

One reason cited for choosing the base scheme over the alternate scheme is the significant premium that would be paid to construct an underground facility for loading and unloading buses. This premium is not thought by some to yield benefits to NCC or NPS commensurate with the added cost. The Volpe Center review was intended to determine if the estimated costs for the proposed schemes are reasonable and accurate, so that decision makers can be confident that the cost data presented can be used in the decision-making process. An estimate for a third scheme was prepared to further aid in the decision-making process.

The design details of both proposed schemes were reviewed, using information provided by NPS, PCF&P and ICI and comparing the designs to common transit bus facility design. The cost estimates were then revised for each to reflect changes to the design that were determined to be appropriate. The design issues for each of the proposed schemes

---

[26] As prepared by International Consultants, Inc. Includes 10% escalation and contingencies of 15% design and 5% construction.
[27] Based on ICI estimate of $605,987 for Basement Level 3 additional parking spaces

are presented below. The cost estimates presented in the following paragraphs include an 8% mark up for general requirements, unless otherwise noted.

Rather than citing each individual reference section and page used for the review and comparison, note that the following references were used extensively:

- RSMeans Square Foot Costs, 21st Annual Edition, R. S. Means Company, Inc.
- RSMeans Environmental Remediation Cost Data – Unit Price, 4th Annual Edition, R. S. Means Company, Inc.
- RSMeans Heavy Construction Cost Data, 10th Annual Edition, R. S. Means Company, Inc.
- Design Guidelines for Bus Transit Systems Using Compressed Natural Gas as an Alternate Fuel, U.S. Department of Transportation, Federal Transit Administration, 1997.

4.1.1. Option 1 (Surface Facility with "DRPA Bridge Triangle" Berths)

The cost breakout for this option was provided by Michael Funk of ICI. The drawings included show twelve bus parking locations in the saw tooth arrangement at the northeast corner of the NCC. This arrangement is slightly different from the eleven-berth arrangement presented to The Volpe Center as Option 1. However, it appears that to include one berth for buses equipped for ADA compliance (the southernmost berth) the designers had to reduce the total berths from twelve to eleven to not extend south beyond the original limit. The cost estimate for the three berths in the Race Street Triangle was not included in the package received from Mr. Funk. These data were later received from Craig Dumas of PCF&P. However, they were not included in the executive summary attached to Mr. Dumas' 9/3/99 letter to Ms. Ros Remer, which is summarized above in Table 4.1.

In addition, there is no cost estimate provided for the overflow area construction that is proposed for 5th Street. This overflow area will require a curb cut, signage and additional site work. Estimated costs for both the DRPA Bridge Triangle spaces and the 5th Street overflow spaces must be included in the total cost for this option. It is assumed that the cost to construct the six stacking spaces on the south side of Race Street will be included in the cost of building the NCC facility, and so are not included here.

4.1.1.1.Surface Work

The ICI estimate of $2,474,124 appears to be reasonable for the saw tooth berth area on the northeast corner of the NCC. Although it is based on 12 berths at the saw tooth site, the removal of one berth and conversion of the southernmost berth to an ADA accessible berth will have little, if any, impact on the cost, and the estimate is valid.

There are two options for the three-berth location in the traffic island on Race Street that is proposed as a pick-up only site as part of the surface scheme. ICI's estimates of $153,895 and $558,571 for the option without and with a canopy, respectively, appear to be reasonable. Note that an addition error of $100 appears in the ICI estimate. These estimated costs include an 8% general requirements increase. In addition, they are escalated and design and construction contingencies are included at different rates form the other construction estimates, which is appropriate for the type of work involved. These different rates are accounted for in Table 4.3 at the end of this section.

There are no cost estimates provided for the construction of overflow spaces on 5th Street. Without details available, it is estimated that this cost is $100,000, based on signage, curb cuts and paving.

4.1.1.2.Surface Work

The ICI estimate of $5,318,067 for the underground car parking portion of the construction of this option appear reasonable.

4.1.2. Option 2 (Underground Facility, no "DRPA Bridge Triangle" Berths)

The facility footprint, from the drawings provided, appears to correspond to the quantities cited in the cost breakout provided by ICI, so it is assumed that the material quantities used in the estimate are accurate.

As designed, the underground facility does not take into account the fact that buses will be fueled by compressed natural gas.[28] A high release rate gas leak from a bus in the facility could create an explosion hazard. CNG is stored aboard buses at up to 3,500 psi in cylinders located either on the roof or under the floor. Recent events at various locations where CNG is used indicate that a high percentage of fuel leak incidents occur when buses are parked after being operated, which is the type of operation that will occur in this facility if it is built. All possible methane accumulation locations and potential ignition sources must be identified and addressed. Additionally, methane detection systems, proper forced ventilation and emergency notification and evacuation plans must be considered.

4.1.2.1.Surface Work

The ICI estimate for the surface work for Option 2 is $1,932,903. This estimate appears to be reasonable for the design as presented, but as noted above, the design omits consideration of CNG fueled buses, which is estimated later.

4.1.2.2.Underground Work

The design as presented was reviewed first, and then considerations for CNG were made.

All construction work appears to be accurately estimated as presented in the ICI estimates of the PCF&P drawings. There is nothing in the prepared estimates that is in conflict

---

[28] Although nearly all road coaches are now diesel fueled, that is changing. One out of four transit buses built today is CNG fueled, and as emissions standards are tightened, a significant percentage of road coaches will be CNG fueled, also. Liquefied Natural Gas (LNG) will not be widely used, so is not included in this report.

with any of the drawings available for this review. However, it appears that the people-moving machinery is underestimated, as described below.

This design proposes two escalators – one up and one down, presumably – to carry people between the bus parking level and the main floor of the NC Center. The amount estimated to be $450,000 appears reasonable. However, the design proposes one elevator (2-stop, 1-floor, 1-sided) with accompanying enclosure at a cost of $297,500. Assuming a hydraulic elevator, which is standard for this type of installation, a more reasonable estimate would be $225,000. It is not believed, however, that a single elevator is sufficient to handle the passenger load, many of whom are elderly or have limited mobility and prefer elevators to escalators. The design should include four elevators ganged in the same area. The cost of the four elevators is estimated to be $600,000 (4 elevators + 2.5 times the enclosure cost.

The ICI estimate includes a line item of $50,000 for Control booth/Gates. No provision appears to be included for video equipment, computers, communications and other similar items required to make this scheme work operationally. An estimate of the cost for these items is $100,000.

These changes increase the estimate for underground work to $7,351,766.

Combining the original surface and revised underground estimates and adding 8% general requirements increases the total estimate to $9,284,669, or an increase of $434,700 over the ICI estimated cost.

4.1.2.3. Underground Car Parking

The ICI estimate of $5,857,938 for the car parking portion of the facility appears to be reasonable. The deletion of $456,230 if no level B-3 parking is included also appears reasonable.

4.1.2.4. CNG Considerations

As the number of CNG fueled buses increases, there is a higher likelihood of a CNG-related incident occurring in the proposed underground bus facility. A prudent design must account for the operation of CNG fueled buses. The proposed design includes features that will make it difficult, at best, to incorporate recommended design provisions to mitigate the fire and explosion risk associated with CNG fueled buses. When handled properly and in a facility that is designed appropriately, CNG presents no greater risk than diesel fueled buses. However, improper handling or design can result in serious situations arising. Some design considerations recommended to make the facility CNG friendly are:

- Beam – Ceiling Design: Possibly the most restrictive design feature of the proposed underground facility is the use of tall profile concrete ceiling/floor beams. This type of design provides numerous pockets where methane, which is lighter than air, can accumulate. In the event of a high release rate leak from a bus parked in this facility, methane (CNG is 82-97% methane) will rapidly accumulate in these overhead pockets. An ignition possibility occurs within the flammability limits of 5-15% volume of CNG in air. In order to minimize the potential of methane concentrating up to the point where it falls within the lower and upper flammability limits, the beams, trusses and purlins should be "open" design. Alternatively, airtight ceiling panels could be used to close the pockets, although this option would significantly increase the cost of methane detection equipment required and significantly complicate the forced ventilation routing.

- Methane Detection: Methane detectors should be located in all areas where it is likely that methane gas can accumulate as a result of either a high or low release rate leak from a CNG fueled bus parked in the facility. The design proposed for Option 2 would require numerous such detectors. Detectors should be considered to automatically initiate appropriate responses if methane is detected at 20% of the lower flammability limit (1% volume in air) at any location in the facility.

- Forced Ventilation: In the event of a detection (see above), exhaust fans should be automatically operated, in conjunction with vents, louvers, etc., to provide adequate ventilation to effectively eliminate pockets of methane that can reach the lower flammability limit. The proposed design includes forced ventilation, but does not address stagnant pockets. Additionally, all fans, blowers and other equipment should be National Electric Code Class 1, Division 2 certified, since they will be operating in a gas rich environment in the event of a leak.

- Electrical Equipment: All spark generating equipment should be de-energized in the event of a leak. All electrical equipment in the travel path of the gas rich air should be investigated and appropriate measures taken to eliminate, relocate or replace it with appropriate equipment. The National Fire Protection Association's NFPA 52 and applicable parts of NFPA 70 should be adhered to.

- Emergency Systems: Detection of methane should, in addition to energizing ventilation, automatically sound appropriate audible alarms, display visual alarms and summon necessary personnel at the facility and from appropriate emergency response agencies, such as police and fire.

It is impossible to determine actual costs for the design changes that would need to be incorporated into the design of the underground facility to make it CNG friendly. However, experience with costs to transit properties across the country indicates that the approximate cost of making the necessary changes to this facility would probably fall in the range of $2M to $5M. For the purpose of comparisons between the different options presented for the National Constitution Center, an estimate of $3,500,000 should be appropriate.

4.1.3. Option 3A (16 Saw Tooth Berths at NCC)

This option is the preferred *transportation* solution recommended by the Volpe Center. Option 3a comprises sixteen berths located linearly in the saw tooth area at NCC. Additional berths will require that the exit ramp from the saw tooth area onto 5th Street be relocated south of the triangular corner of the NCC building. While aware of the sensitivity of intruding into the green space of this area, The Volpe Center believes that a "designer barrier" can be constructed that will ensure that bus passengers waiting in this area will not be adversely affected by sight, noise or exhaust from buses leaving the facility. The barrier can also be designed to be visually integrated with the NCC building and the green space south of it. It is anticipated that the circular barrier would carry the roofline of the building throughout its length. The barrier could be integrated into the park, by using it as a mural wall for student pictures, display for patriotic scenes and similar uses.

The 16 berths will accommodate nearly all existing bus activity at the ITC. In the event that it becomes necessary to construct additional overload berths to handle increased peak traffic, The Volpe Center recommends that the overflow spaces be relocated from 5th Street to two different locations on 6th Street. This additional work can be studied in more detail as the need arises. The appendices contain more detailed data on the overflow spaces.

The cost of this option is estimated as a variation of Option 1. Assuming that 16 berths are built (this is the maximum possible with all berths north of the corner of the NCC building) is a 45.5% increase over the 11 berths of Option 1. ICI's estimate for surface work is increased by this percentage, after subtracting out $227,510 for the NCC Building items and other items common to both designs. Adding to this the estimate of $200,000 for construction of a designer barrier between the bus exit and the green space and adding the 8% general requirement results in an estimate for this option of $3,488,053.

The cost of constructing five overflow berths on 6th Street is not included in this estimate, as they will not be built as part of this initial phase.

Adding to this the cost of car parking results in the total estimate of $8,806,120.

4.1.4. Option 3B (11 Saw Tooth, 2 Race Street, 3 ITC Berths)

This option is the next preferred (second-best) solution recommended by the Volpe Center. It includes 11 saw tooth berths, as recommended by the architects, while adding five additional berths all within the existing footprint of the ITC. It also satisfies the requirement that all berths be co-located to improve operational management. There are two berths proposed for the south side of Race St., immediately west of the entrance to the underground automobile parking garage. This location is sufficient to allow entrance and exit tapers to maximize safety of buses entering and exiting the spaces on Race Street. Originally, this option included a single space at this location and four ITC berths, but was amended slightly by the architects following the 1/13/00 meeting at NPS, where the concept was proposed. The westernmost edge of the overflow berth also stays far enough east to not intrude into the sight lines of the NCC main entrance on 6th Street. While these berth are not located in the same area as the 11 saw tooth berths, it is just around the corner from the first saw tooth berth, and is essentially part of the same location.

The three additional overflow berths would be located on the eastern most side of the ITC bus berth area. The island will be cut down to a width that is adequate for all passenger and pedestrian movements and relocated consistent with the Philadelphia Streets Department agreement to relinquish some of 5th Street to the facility. Although the length of this island would permit 6 or 7 buses to park there, the 3 berths will be permanently marked, leaving ample room between them to allow any of the 3 to be accessed independently from the others. This will require parallel parking in some cases, but this will not occur on the street, but in the ITC bus yard. Even at worst existing peak times of sixty four buses per hour, the average traffic in the facility is about one bus per minute, allowing ample time for the drivers to make the maneuver. The on-site controllers will also be able to assist in this operation, assuring no conflicts. If the Race Street berths and all eleven saw tooth berths are occupied, the next bus will continue around the turnout and re-enter the ITC yard, instead of exiting onto Race Street. The bus would proceed to the northernmost berth on the island. Subsequent buses will fill the spaces behind the first bus. A more detailed explanation of turning/backing movement conflicts is presented in the appendices.

In the few instances where all sixteen berths are full (4% of Spring weekday peak times) a bus controller at the south end of the yard will instruct the driver to perform the "go around" maneuver. This would require the driver to exit onto 5th Street, turn right on Race Street, Right on 4th Street, right on Arch Street, right on 5th Street, and return into the ITC Yard overflow entrance via a left turn. The controllers will either hold the bus momentarily or direct it into one of the four overflow berths. This route is the least intrusive of all of the overflow travel schemes investigated; it entails circling one city block, versus several with all of the other overflow paths proposed. Alternately, overflow buses could be directed to the overflow berths, currently proposed for 5th Street, but recommended by The Volpe Center on 6th Street. By proper management of the facility, specifically better coordination with tour groups and schools, it is probable that the sixteen berths will be adequate for all existing traffic at the ITC.

A cantilevered overhang with a vertical wall on the easternmost side of the new island is proposed to protect passengers and provide visual screening of the ITC facility from the 5th Street side. This structure would be similar in nature to the canopy proposed by the architect for the DRPA Bridge Triangle spaces. There will also be sufficient room for landscaping treatments along 5th Street.

The cost to construct this sixteen berth arrangement will be slightly higher than the scheme proposed by the architect that includes the DRPA Bridge Triangle berths. The base cost is the same as the eleven saw tooth berth option with no overflow, which is $7,792,191. Added to this is the cost to construct the 2 berths on Race Street, which is estimated to be $100,000, including the 8% general requirements.

The canopy over the 5th Street island will be approximately 5200 square feet and the eastern wall will be approximately 3200 square feet, for a total structure slightly more than twice the size of the one proposed for the DRPA Bridge Triangle. This estimated cost is $867,181, including the 8% general requirements.

The estimated cost of this option, including 8% general requirements but not including contingencies or escalation, is $8,759,372.

4.1.5. Option 3C (11 Saw Tooth, 3 Race Street, 3 Triangle Berths)

Orth Rodgers submitted another design option following the meeting at NPS on 1/13/00. This option includes the original 11 saw tooth berths at NCC, 2 berths on Race Street. While this newly proposed option differs dramatically from the original Option 1 on which it is based, the differences are primarily in operations, and not in construction. Therefore, it is estimated that the construction costs for this new option will be the same as for Option 1(d), which included a canopy over the three DRPA Bridge Triangle berths. This cost, including the 8% general requirements, is $8,450,762.

4.1.6. Option 4 (Revised 14 Saw Tooth, 2 Race Street Berths)

Following a meeting in Philadelphia on January 13, 2000, it was learned that the City of Philadelphia Department of Streets would be willing to allow the ITC to extend eastward into Fifth Street by a dimension which based on subsequent lane reconfiguration and adjustment has turned out to be 26'-4". This extension has allowed for the satisfactory redesign of the original Option 4, the initial version of which had been rejected due to safety concerns with bus movements. The new Option 4 as redesigned and as presented herein eliminates the six stacking spaces on Race Street and replaces them with two berths between 6th Street and the entrance to the underground NCC parking garage. The 11 saw tooth berths remain on the east side of the NCC building, and the original 4 shallow saw tooth berths on the eastern side of the ITC lot are replaced by 3 shallow saw tooth berths located in the same area. The island containing the three shallow saw tooth berths is relocated eastward to reflect the additional 5th Street area taken up. There are no DRPA Bridge Triangle berths included with this option. Overflow spaces are assumed to remain on 5th Street.

4.1.6.1.Surface Work

The eleven saw tooth berths will cost the same as for Option 1, estimated at $2,474,124. Additional work in the ITC lot to construct the three shallow saw tooth berths, including additional work to the island and crosswalks, is estimated to cost $150,000. This cost does not include any type of canopy to protect passengers in this area, as none is shown in the drawing received from PCF&P. The cost of a canopy and wall, similar to Option 3B, would cost $867,181, including the 8% general requirements.

There are no cost estimates provided for the construction of overflow spaces on 5th Street. Without details available, it is estimated that this cost is $100,000, based on signage, curb cuts and paving.

It is assumed that the cost to construct the three spaces on the south side of Race Street will be included in the cost of building the NCC facility, and so are not included here. The total estimate for Option 4 surface work is then $3,591,305.

4.1.6.2.Underground Car Parking

The ICI estimate of $5,318,067 for the underground car parking portion of the construction of Option 1 will not change under this option.

The total estimate for Option 4, including 8% general requirements, is $8,909,372.

4.1.7. Summary of Cost Estimates

Table 4.1.2 summarizes the estimated costs of the various options proposed. Due to the lack of cost data included in the original material reviewed by The Volpe Center, several different variations of the first two options are presented. The final estimates, including escalation and contingencies, for each of the options proposed is listed in Table 4.1.3. Two tables are required because all options and variations use a general requirements mark-up of 8%, while there are different contingency rates for different construction items.

Table 4.1.2. Summary of Construction Cost Estimates

Design Option	Description	Estimate[29]
Option 1a	Surface bus with car parking, 11 saw tooth berths, no overflow cost	7,792,191
Option 1b (Revised)	Surface bus with car parking, 11 saw tooth berths, overflow on 5th Street	7,892,191
Option1c (Revised)	Same as 1b plus 3 DRPA Bridge Triangle berths without canopy	8,046,086
Option 1d (Revised)	Same as 1b plus 3 DRPA Bridge Triangle berths with canopy	8,450,762
Option 2a (PCF&P)	Underground, 16 berths, no Level B-3 Parking	14,251,677
Option 2b (PCF&P)	Underground, 16 berths, with Level B-3 parking	14,707,907
Option 2c (Revised)	Same as 2a, costs revised by Volpe	14,686,377
Option 2d (Revised)	Same as 2b, costs revised by Volpe	15,142,607
Option 2e (New)	Same as 2c, Includes CNG designs	18,186,377
Option 2f (New)	Same as 2d, Includes CNG designs	18,642,607
Option 3A (New)	Surface bus with car parking, 16 saw tooth berths, no overflow	8,806,120
Option 3B (New)	Surface bus with car parking, 11 saw tooth berths, 2 Race St. berth, 3 "overflow" berths at ITC	8,759,372
Option 3C (New)	Surface bus with car parking, 11 saw tooth berths, 3 Race Street berths, 3 DRPA Bridge Triangle berths	8,450,762
Option 4 (New)	Re-designed with car parking, 11 saw tooth berths, 3 shallow saw tooth berths[30], 3 Race St. berths	8,909,372

---

[29] Estimate includes 8% General Requirements, but does not include escalation, design contingency or construction contingency.

Table 4.1.3. Summary of *Total* Construction Cost Estimates

Design Option	Description	Estimate	Total[31]
Option 1a	Surface bus with car parking, 11 saw tooth berths, no overflow cost	7,792,191	10,349,978
Option 1b (Revised)	Surface bus with car parking, 11 saw tooth berths, overflow on 5th St.	7,892,191	10,482,803
Option1c (Revised)	Same as 1b plus 3 DRPA Bridge Triangle berths without canopy	8,046,086	10,218,529
Option 1d (Revised)	*Same as 1b plus 3 DRPA Bridge Triangle berths with canopy*	*8,450,762*	*10,732,467*
Option 2a (PCF&P)	Underground, 16 berths, no Level B-3 Parking	14,251,677	18,929,790
Option 2b (PCF&P)	Underground, 16 berths, with Level B-3 parking	14,707,907	19,535,777
Option 2c (Revised)	Same as 2a, costs revised by Volpe	14,686,377	19,507,180
Option 2d (Revised)	Same as 2b, costs revised by Volpe	15,142,607	20,113,168
Option 2e (New)	*Same as 2c, Includes CNG designs*	*18,186,377*	*24,156,055*
Option 2f (New)	*Same as 2d, Includes CNG designs*	*18,642,607*	*24,762,043*
Option 3A (New)	Surface bus with car parking, up to 16 saw tooth berths, overflow on 6th Street (2 locations)	8,806,120	11,696,729
Option 3B (New)	*Surface bus with car parking, 11 saw tooth berths, 1 Race St. berth, 4 overflow spaces in ITC bus area*	*8,759,372*	*11,634,636*
Option 3C (New)	*Surface bus with car parking, 11 saw tooth berths, 3 Race Street berths, 3 DRPA Bridge Triangle berths*	*8,450,762*	*10,732,467*
Option 4 (New)	*Re-designed with car parking, 11 saw tooth berths, 3 shallow saw tooth berths[32], 3 Race St. berths*	*8,909,372*	*11,314,902*

---

[30] No canopy is proposed to cover the three shallow saw tooth berths on the east side of the ITC lot.

[31] Includes 10% escalation, 15% design contingency and 5% construction contingency for all items except Options 1c and 1d. These options use 8% escalation, 12% design contingency and 5% construction contingency for the costs associated with the DRPA Bridge Triangle berths, and 10%, 15% and 5% for the remaining items.

[32] No canopy is proposed to cover the three shallow saw tooth berths on the east side of the ITC lot.

4.2. Operations Staffing Estimates

The Volpe Center reviewed the draft bus management plan prepared by Abrams-Cherwony (AC) for Option 1. No management plan for Option 2 was received, although very brief discussions of how to manage the underground bus facility were held at a meeting in Philadelphia on December 3, 1999.

While the staffing levels for Option 1 correspond to what The Volpe Center recommends for Option 3b, the benefits and overhead calculations of the AC draft appear to be significantly below what can be expected for this type of operation. The part of the AC draft plan that appears to be most at odds with anticipated staffing requirements for the ITC facility is the salary amounts projected for the positions to be staffed. The AC equipment estimates appear to be reasonable for the implementation of Option 1, with the exception, that the annunciation system specified could be enhanced, at higher cost.

The Volpe Center believes that for the ITC to function properly, positions within the facility must be staffed by professionals who will be adequately compensated. A large percentage of visitors to the NCC and other parts of Independence Park will arrive on buses, and it is critical for the facility to operate smoothly and continue to refine operations to provide the most pleasant and efficient process possible. This policy is directly in line with the stated desire of NCC to provide a high quality experience for visitors to this important national treasure.

4.2.1. Staffing Costs

Estimates for the annual payroll costs to operate the ITC facility will vary considerably between different schemes and designs. The estimate presented here is that which is deemed appropriate to staff the ITC defined in Option 3b as prepared by the Volpe Center. The necessary positions are:

- ITC Manager - Responsible for the overall operation of the facility. Serves as the primary liaison with NCC and NPS to ensure that ITC role is accepted. Prepares reports and makes presentations as necessary. Researches operations world-wide and brings knowledge to bear on improvements to the ITC facility and operations.
- Assistant Manager/Head Controller – Responsible for the day-to-day operations, training and maintenance of the facility. Fills in as needed to control buses and greet passengers.
- Head Greeter – Responsible for protocol, staffing, scheduling, and overseeing the greeter function. May serve as controller if needed. Fills in for clerk as needed.
- Controller – Directs bus movements into, out of and within the ITC facility. Serves as Greeter if needed. Fills in for clerk as needed. Obtains necessary information from tour guides/teachers/bus drivers as needed and enters it into the database.
- Greeter – Meets bus passengers and obtains necessary data from tour guides/teachers/drivers and enters it into the database. Guides pedestrian movements throughout the ITC facility.

70

- <u>Clerk</u> – Performs all routine office functions. Answers phones and handles all mail and other correspondence. Enters data into database. Makes announcements as necessary. Operates Base radio for communications with other staff.

The position descriptions above are general in nature, and will need to be expanded significantly to generate position descriptions to be used for actual staffing purposes. As envisioned, there will be overlap between positions to allow for flexibility in handling staffing shortages that may arise from emergency, sickness, scheduling conflicts and other occurrences that may affect the operation of the ITC. For example, in the morning, when it is probable that the four overflow berths will not be needed, the controllers will be free to serve as greeters. This will provide a better experience for the arriving passengers. In the afternoon, when the controllers will be busy directing buses through the facility and into the four overflow berths, this greeting function will not be as important, and the controllers will focus on the bus movements while the greeters handle the outgoing passengers.

For this and other reasons, it will be imperative to fill the top positions with qualified, dedicated professionals who are able to inspire the ITC workforce to operate in a cooperative and productive manner. The estimated salary costs to staff the ITC are listed in Table 4.2.1.

Table 4.2.1. ITC Staffing and Annual Salary Requirements for Option 3B.

Position	Number	Annual Rate	Salary
ITC Manager	1	65,000	$ 65,000
Assistant Manager (Head Controller)	1	55,000	$ 55,000
Head Greeter	1	35,000	$ 35,000
F.T. Controller	2	35,000	$ 70,000
F.T. Greeter	2	25,000	$ 50,000
F.T. Clerk	1	25,000	$ 25,000
P.T. Controller	1	10,000	$ 10,000
P.T. Greeter	4	7,000	$ 28,000
P.T. Clerk	1	12,500	$ 12,500
Full Time Staff	8		$ 300,000
Part Time Staff	6		$ 50,500
Total Staff	**14**		$ 350,500
		Benefits @ 25%	$ 87,625
		Overhead @ 25%	$ 109,531
		Total Annual Salary	**$ 547,656**

In addition to the staffing costs, there are other costs associated with operating the ITC facility. These costs can be broken down into equipment costs for installing the operating systems in the facility and annual equipment costs for maintenance, repair and replacement of equipment and other annual operating costs for items like cleaning, supplies, and similar requirements.

4.2.2. Initial Equipment Costs

ITC facility equipment costs will vary according to the design and operating plan. This estimate is based on Option 3b. It includes a state-of-the-art information system that will function to expedite passenger and bus movements and minimize dwell times associated with dropping off and (especially) picking up passengers at the ITC. As envisioned, there will be video and audio announcement equipment strategically located for all visitors traveling through the ITC. Information will be input into the system via hand held devices that can also be used to retrieve bus data and at the central control in the ITC office. As a bus drops off passengers, the bus will be assigned a number uniquely identifying it to the system. The bus driver will be instructed to display this number, on a placard, in the bus windshield. The clerk will enter the tour group name, school name, etc. into the database. When returning to pick up passengers at the ITC, a controller will input the bus number into the system, along with the berth the bus will enter, as soon as it is determined where the bus will stop. This data will then be correlated by the system to the tour/school information and displayed on the video boards. A computer-generated audio announcement will also be made.

In the event of a failure of the system, the clerk and Assistant Manager will manually manage the data and make the announcements.

Estimated costs to purchase and install the necessary equipment are listed in Table 4.2.2.

4.2.3. Annual Equipment Costs

There will be relatively small equipment costs associated with operating the ITC facility. These costs include equipment repair and replacement, upgrades, and other similar expenses. It is estimated that these costs will be budgeted at $30,000 per year.

4.2.4. Annual Supplies Costs

The annual cost to operate the ITC facility includes such items as mailing fees, postage, office supplies, batteries, and other nominal items. The largest cost for supplies will be for cleaning, maintenance and replacement/repair of the staff uniforms. The staff will be outfitted in appropriate uniforms and will require sufficient foul weather gear to maintain operations in all types of inclement weather. The estimated cost for supplies is $35,000.

The total annual operating cost is includes salaries, equipment and supplies, as noted above. A summary of the total annual operating costs expected for the ITC under Option 3B is given in Table 4.2.3.

Table 4.2.2. Initial Equipment Costs for Option 3b, ITC Facility

Item	Quantity	Unit Cost	Total Cost
Cell Phones	3	150	$ 450
Radios (Field)	14	100	$ 1,400
Base Radio	1	5000	$ 5,000
Office Phone System	1	7500	$ 7,500
Office Furniture	1	10000	$ 10,000
Surveillance Camera	3	3500	$ 10,500
TV Monitor	1	2000	$ 2,000
Computer	2	3000	$ 6,000
Printer	2	600	$ 1,200
Copier	1	500	$ 500
Facsimile Machine	1	500	$ 500
Software	1	10000	$ 10,000
Passenger Notification System			
Video Displays	4	14000	$ 56,000
Voice Announcement System	1	50000	$ 50,000
Hand-held Input/Output Device	16	1500	$ 24,000
Central Control	1	5000	$ 5,000
Safety Equipment	1	5000	$ 5,000
Signage	1	10000	$ 10,000
Vehicle (EZ GO type)	1	10000	$ 10,000
Men's/Women's Lockers	16	1000	$ 16,000
Uniforms and Foul Weather Gear	16	500	$ 8,000
Equipment Subtotal			$ 239,050
Contingency		10%	$ 23,905
Equipment Total			**$ 262,955**

Table 4.2.3. Total Annual Operating Costs, Option 3b, ITC Facility

Item	Cost	
Staff Salaries (Fully Loaded)	$	547,656
Equipment	$	30,000
Supplies	$	35,000
Total	**$**	**612,656**

The annual operating cost of $612, 656 for Option 3b can be compared to estimates for the other options.

- Option 1

  This option would be the most labor intensive of the options available, because all buses are stopped at the stacking location on Race Street before they can proceed to the ITC. Controllers would be required at the stacking lanes and in the facility. The Abrams-Cherwony plan identifies 14 persons to staff this option, but it appears that this number would be low by perhaps four part time controllers. Also, due to the complexity of pre-scheduling pick ups and drop offs, additional staffing will be needed to coordinate with the tour bus companies and the schools. This effort could require two more part time clerks. The additional staff The Volpe Center believes will be necessary to operate Option 1 would be higher than that for Option 3b by these additional six employees and the associated costs for them. The estimated costs for the additional staff and equipment are $101,560 and $10,000, respectively.

- Option 2

  Staffing Levels for Option 2 would be lower than that for Option 3b. With all of the buses arriving at the central location of an underground facility, where all berths are arranged around a central platform. There would be fewer controllers required to operate this scheme. Since there are sixteen berths at this facility, the overflow berths are not needed for virtually all of the time of operation, with the exception of a few buses in the afternoon on spring weekdays. Therefore, controllers will seldom be required to meet buses at the overflow spaces. The number of part time staff could be reduced by two greeters and their associated costs, or $59,000.

- Option 3a

  Option 3a is the most operationally simple plan for handling buses at the ITC. All of the berths are located at the facility in an arrangement that makes the First Come First Serve regimen work well. Sixteen berths also are enough to handle all current bus arrivals with the exception of a few buses in the afternoon of spring weekdays. Due to the simplicity of operation, the staff could be reduced by one full time controller and one full time greeter. This would reduce the salaries and equipment costs by $96,750.

75

- Option 4

    It is estimated that Option 4 operating costs will be the same as for Option 3b.

A summary of estimated total annual operating costs for all options is shown in Table 4.2.4.

Table 4.2.4. Total Annual Operating Costs

Option	Total Annual Operating Cost
Option One	$724,216
Option Two	$553,656
Option Three A	$515,906
Option Three B	$612,656
Option Four	$612,656

5. Summary Recommendations

Given the vast amount of material, and the complexity of the issues, it is not an easy task to provide a concise decision-making framework for identifying a preferred design option or options. The Volpe Center team believes, however, that the results of analysis of each of the six options allow the following observations and recommendations to be made.

5.1. Options Removed from Further Consideration

The Volpe Center analysis of the options proposed indicates that Option 1[33], Option 2[34] and Option 3C[35] have issues associated with them that make them less desirable than the remaining options. Sections 2.2 through 2.7 explain the issues in detail. It is recommended that these three options be removed from further consideration. This leaves Option 3A, Option 3B, and Option 4 to consider as preferred designs.

5.2. Option 3A

This option clearly dominates on all technical evaluative criteria, except for the fact that it may violate an architectural/building line/view corridor constraint. The Volpe Center's ideal recommendation is to conduct further architectural and landscape studies to see whether Option 3A can fit within the NCC and Park environment without adverse impacts (e.g., scale of facility and wall to NCC structure, light and shadow effects of designer wall, views into and out of the park towards the ITC facility, connection to the NCC building roofline, etc., etc.). If these studies indicate little or no adverse impact, the Volpe Center recommends implementation of Option 3A.

However, if extending the ITC beyond the NCC building line seems to be a "hard" site constraint that can not be violated, and the stakeholders who control the decision are resolute on this, it is recommended that Option 3A also be removed from further consideration.

5.3. Option 3B

The elevation data provided by PCF&P raises the question of whether Option 3B is feasible, due to an area of 12.75% grade on the ramp that re-enters the ITC bus aisle. At question is whether buses can negotiate the up-grade ramp after the turnaround back into the ITC facility to access what the Volpe Center showed as the three quasi overflow bus berths.

The Volpe Center made a scaled template of the design vehicle ("typical" 45 foot tour bus) and conducted simulated movements of a bus negotiating the ramp with the vertical road profile as indicated by the PCF drawings. While it is tight with respect to the

---

[33] Issues include stacking overflow on Race Street, a complex management system and use of the DRPA Bridge Triangle berths.

[34] Issues include failure to account for CNG designs and lack of ability to remove disabled buses.

[35] Issues include use of the DRPA Bridge Triangle berths which may result in interlocking queues under different scenarios.

approach, breakover and departure angles of the vehicle, the bus can negotiate the ramp. This is an important finding. Furthermore, the bus would approach the ramp after the turnaround in a skewed angle, which effectively lowers the effective grade that is negotiated (longer distance over the same elevation). School buses have significantly higher approach, break over and departure angles than do the tour buses, so they will negotiate the ramp with no difficulty. One suggestion might be to include a guideline marking of dotted lines on the up-ramp to encourage this approach angle by the buses. Another design suggestion is to include a small embankment wall to separate the northern entry to the turnaround from the southern re-entry. This would permit different grades for the two ramps, with the ramp back into the ITC at a lowered grade. With the widening of the ITC bus aisle afforded by the additional 12 feet of 5th Street, there appears to be enough room at the southern end of the bus aisle to permit this.

This ramp angle may serve a beneficial purpose, in that buses will be forced to slowly transverse it. Since there are two pedestrian crossings flanking the ramp, buses moving more slowly is a plus.

Option 3B releases buses (from berths #14, #15 and #16) onto Race Street, immediately west of the 5th Street intersection, which is currently signalized. There is no technical difficulty in doing this. It could be done without any adverse impact on traffic flows on Race Street or 5th Street. It could even be done without technically changing the signal to a three-phase signal, or violating the City's hesitancy to do so, as expressed at the 1/13/00 meeting by the Philadelphia Streets Department. If this is a "soft" site constraint and it is negotiable with the City, then Option 3B is the preferred design option. If this is a "hard" constraint, and all vehicles *must* exit the ITC facility onto 5th Street, then Option 3B would be removed from further consideration, and the next best alternative becomes Option 4, with the Volpe Center suggested design modifications included as listed below.

5.4. Option 4

As pointed out in Section 2.7, this option as originally proposed required five design modifications, above and beyond the 26'-4" extension of the eastern curb into Fifth Street, before it was able to be considered workable or operational. These five suggested design modifications were:

- incorporation of a curb extension at 6th Street and Race to protect the "no thru traffic" lane which is the bus access lane to bus berths sited on the southern edge of Race Street;
- locating two (2), not three (3), bus berths, each of 90+ ft. and permitting independent entry and exit, on the southern edge of Race Street;
- adoption of the simplified bus management and control system with the FCFS regimen which would assure that the first 13 bus berths (2 on Race Street, and 11 adjacent to the NCC) are occupied first before the three (3) shallow saw-toothed overflow berths are utilized; and
- allocation of the additional footage created by the eastward extension primarily to the central bus aisle (11 ft for the central bus aisle, and 1 ft for the island platform on the eastern edge of the ITC.)

- Redesigning the NCC walkway on the Western side of the ITC, next to the building or renegotiating with the City to find more space on 5th Street so the island platform on the eastern edge of the ITC can be at least 15 feet wide.

Note that all but the last modification has been accomplished with the redesign; and the eastern walkway is approximately 13 rather than 15 feet.

With the above changes having been incorporated into Option 4, this option becomes the second best option.

Regardless of which Option is selected, both the physical and operational management designs should be field tested in a full scale mock up, using large buses and average drivers.

6. Appendices

6.5. Appendix A, 14-Berth ITC Transactions Per Hour

6.5.1. Spring Weekday (Peak Season)

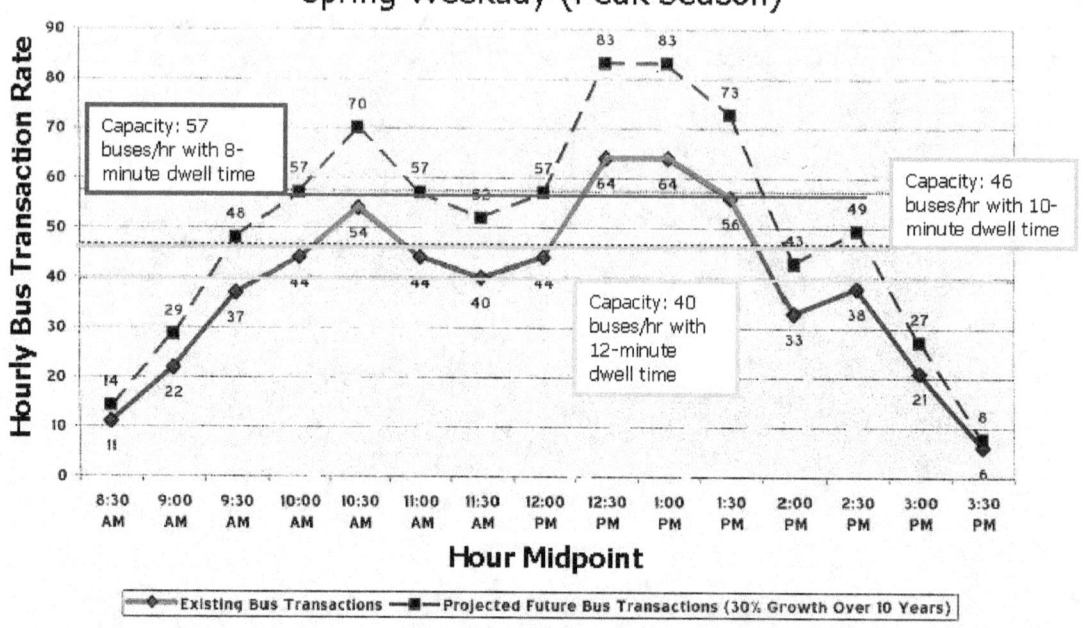

Source:
Orth-Rodgers & Associates, Inc.
Philadelphia, Pennsylvania 19102

6.5.2. Spring, fall, Thanksgiving Weekend, and Christmas Week

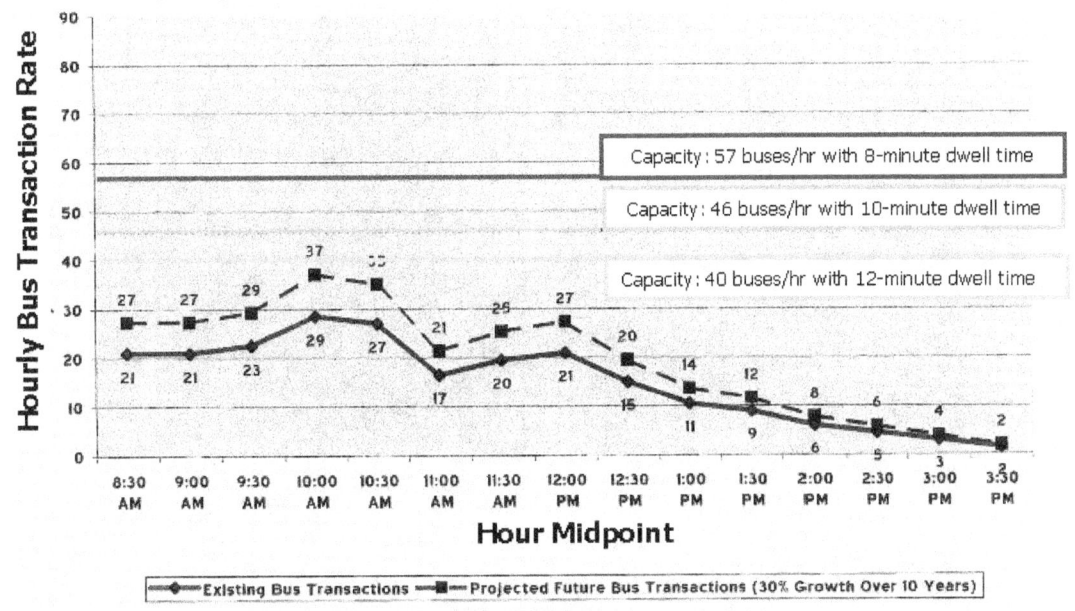

Existing and Future 14-Berth ITC Transactions Per Hour Spring/Fall/Thanksgiving Weekend, Christmas Week

Source:
Orth-Rodgers & Associates, Inc.
Philadelphia, Pennsylvania 19102

6.5.3. Summer

Existing and Future 14-Berth ITC Transactions Per Hour
Summer

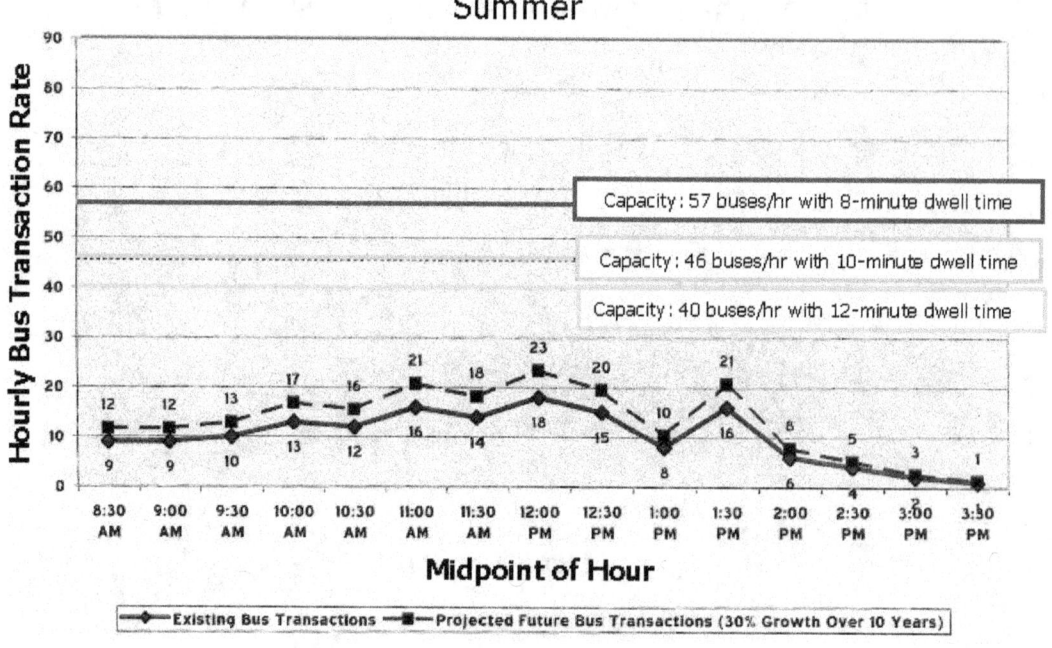

Source:
Orth-Rodgers & Associates, Inc.
Philadelphia, Pennsylvania 19102

6.5.4. Fall Weekday

Existing and Future 14-Berth ITC Transactions Per Hour

Fall Weekday

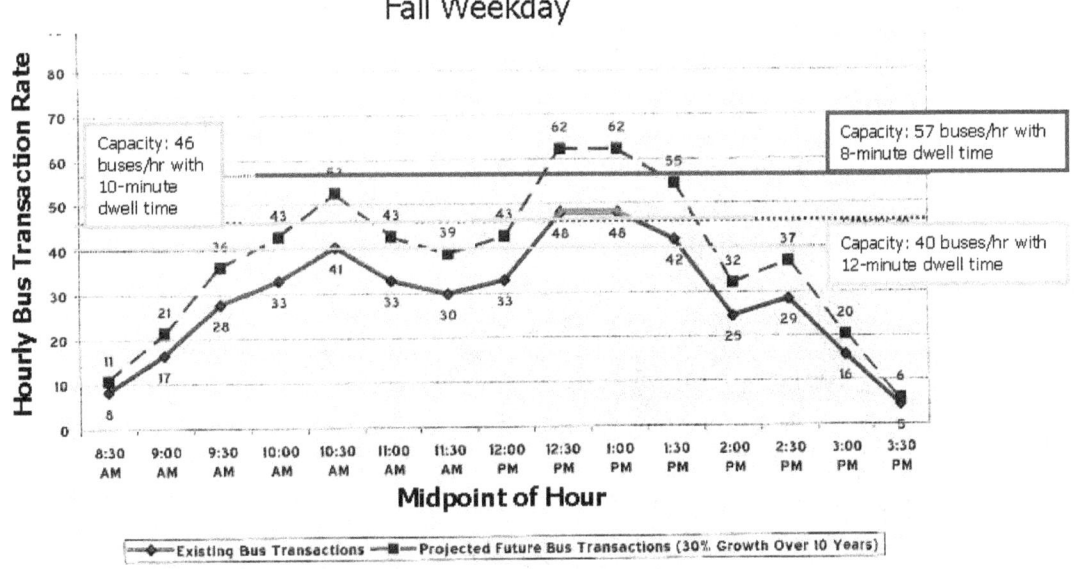

Source:
Orth-Rodgers & Associates, Inc.
Philadelphia, Pennsylvania 19102

83

6.5.5. Comparison Per Season

Comparison of 14-Berth ITC Bus Facility Adequacy Per Season

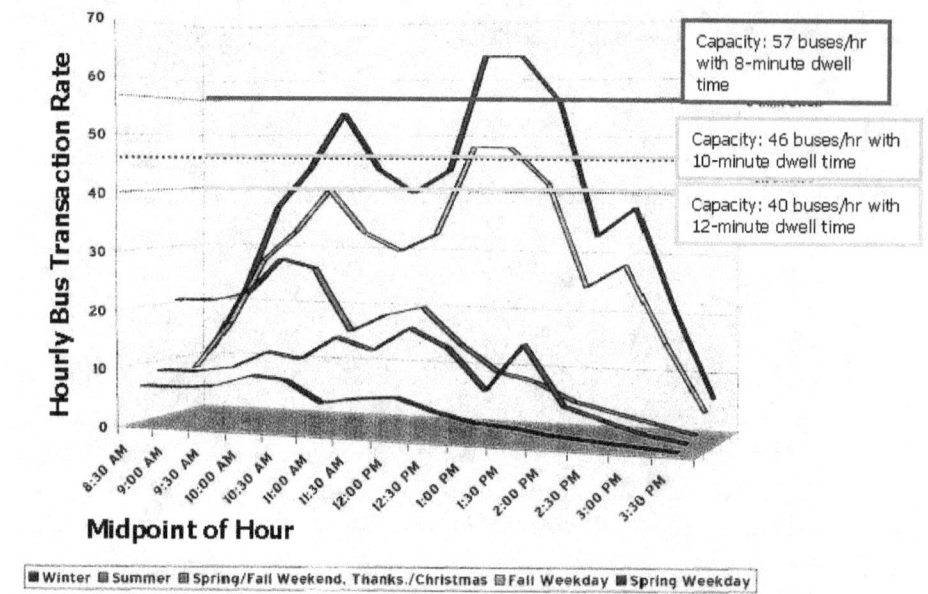

Source:
Orth-Rodgers & Associates, Inc.
Philadelphia, Pennsylvania 19102

6.6. Appendix B, Probability of Overflow

6.6.1. Mean Dwell Time of Eight Minutes

Table 6.6.1. Probability of Overflow (P (n>N)): Mean Dwell Time = 8 Minutes

N=Berths	Mean Bus Arrival Rate (λ) (Buses per hour)				
	40	50	60	70	80
11	0.01	0.06	0.18	0.43	0.86
12	0.00	0.02	0.09	0.25	0.54
13	0.00	0.01	0.05	0.14	0.33
14	0.00	0.00	0.02	0.07	0.19
15	0.00	0.00	0.01	0.04	0.11
16	0.00	0.00	0.00	0.02	0.06
21	0.00	0.00	0.00	0.00	0.00

Calculations based on equations below:

$$P_0 = 1/\Sigma^{N-1}\rho^n/n! + \rho^N/ N!(1-\rho/N)$$

$$P_{n>N} = P_0 [\rho^{N+1}/ N!N(1-\rho/N)$$

6.6.2. Mean Dwell Time of Ten Minutes

Table 6.6.2. Probability of Overflow (P (n>N)): Mean Dwell Time = 10 Minutes

N=Berths	Mean Bus Arrival Rate (λ) (Buses per hour)				
	40	50	60	70	80
11	0.06	0.22	0.62	N/A	N/A
12	0.02	0.12	0.37	0.87	N/A
13	0.01	0.06	0.22	0.55	N/A
14	0.00	0.03	0.12	0.35	0.76
15	0.00	0.01	0.07	0.21	0.50
16	0.00	0.00	0.04	0.12	0.32
21	0.00	0.00	0.00	0.00	0.02

Calculations based on equations below:

$$P_0 = 1/\Sigma^{N-1}\rho^n/n! + \rho^N/N!(1-\rho/N)$$

$$P_{n>N} = P_0 [\rho^{N+1}/N!N(1-\rho/N)$$

6.6.3. Mean Dwell Time of Twelve Minutes

Table 6.6.3. Probability of Overflow (P (n>N)): Mean Dwell Time = 12 Minutes

N=Berths	Mean Bus Arrival Rate (λ) (Buses per hour)				
	40	50	60	70	80
11	0.18	0.62	N/A	N/A	N/A
12	0.09	0.37	N/A	N/A	N/A
13	0.05	0.22	0.65	N/A	N/A
14	0.02	0.12	0.41	N/A	N/A
15	0.01	0.07	0.25	0.67	N/A
16	0.00	0.04	0.15	0.44	N/A
21	0.00	0.00	0.01	0.04	0.13

Calculations based on equations below:

$$P_0 = 1/\Sigma^{N-1}\rho^n/n! + \rho^N/ N!(1-\rho/N)$$

$$P_{n>N} = P_0 [\rho^{N+1}/ N!N(1-\rho/N)$$

6.6.4. Mean Dwell Time of Fifteen Minutes

Table 6.6.4. Probability of Overflow (P (n>N)): Mean Dwell Time = 15 Minutes

N=Berths	Mean Bus Arrival Rate (λ) (Buses per hour)				
	40	**50**	**60**	**70**	**80**
11	0.62	N/A	N/A	N/A	N/A
12	0.37	N/A	N/A	N/A	N/A
13	0.22	0.81	N/A	N/A	N/A
14	0.12	0.53	N/A	N/A	N/A
15	0.07	0.33	N/A	N/A	N/A
16	0.04	0.21	0.68	N/A	N/A
21	0.00	0.01	0.07	0.27	0.72

Calculations based on equations below:

$$P_0 = 1/\Sigma^{N-1}\rho^n/n! + \rho^N/ N!(1-\rho/N)$$

$$P_{n>N} = P_0 [\rho^{N+1}/ N!N(1-\rho/N)$$

6.7. Appendix C, 6th Street Overflow Capacity Charts

Table 1, 6th Street Southbound: Capacity (vehicles per hour) and Saturation Rate (percent) Cycle Time (C) equal to 60 seconds[1], Phase split (G/C) equal to 0.50

	Arch and 6th Street		Market and 6th Street		Chestnut and 6th Street	
	A[2]	B[3]	A	B	A	B
Capacity	2400[4]	1600[4]	2400	1600	2400	1600
Saturation Rate	0.37[5]	0.56	0.33[6]	0.50	0.33[7]	0.49

Notes:
1. Orth-Rodgers & Associates Inc. Traffic Data and Analysis: Final Report, p.12.
2. 3 12 ft. general purpose vehicular lanes (N=3)
3. 1 12 ft. + 1 11 ft. general purpose vehicular lanes (N=2)
4. HCM, eq. 11-5, c=1600* N* G/C
5. Based on a service volume flow rate during evening weekday peak hour of 894 vehicles, consisting of right-turns westbound on *Arch*, and through movements southbound on 6th Street; see Orth-Rodgers & Associates Inc., Traffic Data and Analysis: Final Report, 1995, Figure 3.
6. Based on a service volume flow rate during evening weekday peak hour of 796 vehicles, consisting of through movements southbound on *6th Street*, and left and right-turning movements onto *Market* Street (two-way); see Orth-Rodgers & Associates Inc., Traffic Data and Analysis: Final Report, 1995, Figure 3.
7. Based on a service volume flow rate during evening weekday peak hour of 792 vehicles, consisting of through movements southbound on *6th Street*, and left-turning movements onto *Chestnut* Street; see Orth-Rodgers & Associates Inc., Traffic Data and Analysis: Final Report, 1995, Figure 3.

Table 2, 6th Street Southbound: Total Approach Delay (D) (seconds per vehicle) Cycle Time (C) equal to 60 seconds[1], Phase split (G/C) equal to 0.50

	A^2	B^3
Arch and 6th Street	9.1^4	10.7^4
Market and 6th Street	8.7^4	10.1^4
Chestnut and 6th Street	8.5^4	10.1^4

Notes:
1. Orth-Rodgers & Associates Inc., Traffic Data and Analysis: Final Report, p. 12.
2. 3 12 ft. general purpose vehicular lanes (N=3)
3. 1 12 ft. + 1 11 ft. general purpose vehicular lanes (N=2)
4. HCM, eq. 11-2, D=1.3d; d (stopped delay under random vehicle arrivals) given by equation 9-18.

Table 3, 6th Street Southbound: Level of Service (LOS)[1] Cycle Time (C) equal to 60 seconds[2], Phase split (G/C) equal to 0.50

	A^3	B^4
Arch and 6th Street	B^5	B
Market and 6th Street	B^5	B
Chestnut and 6th Street	B^5	B

Notes:
1. Orth-Rodgers & Associates Inc., Traffic Data and Analysis: Final Report, Table 3, from HCM1985, TRB SR 209.
2. Orth-Rodgers & Associates Inc., Traffic Data and Analysis: Final Report, p. 12.
3. 3 12 ft. general purpose vehicular lanes (N=3)
4. 1 12 ft. + 1 11 ft. general purpose vehicular lanes (N=2)
5. Orth-Rodgers & Associates Inc., Traffic Data and Analysis: Final Report, Figure 14.

Table 4, 6th Street Southbound: Mean Queue Length per Lane (vehicles) Cycle Time (C) equal to 60 seconds[1], Phase split (G/C) equal to 0.50

	A[2]	B[3]
Arch and 6th Street	3.0[4]	5.2[4]
Market and 6th Street	2.7[4]	4.4[4]
Chestnut and 6th Street	2.6[4]	4.4[4]

Notes:
1. Orth-Rodgers & Associates Inc., Traffic Data and Analysis: Final Report, p. 12.
2. 3 12 ft. general purpose vehicular lanes (N=3)
3. 1 12 ft. + 1 11 ft. general purpose vehicular lanes (N=2)
4. Calculated from Little's formula, $E(Q) = qR/N - qh$, where q = flow rate (vps), R = the effective red time, N = the number of lanes, and h = saturation flow rate (discharge headway, seconds per vehicle); see W. Ashton, Theory of Road Traffic Flow, 1966, p. 125.

Table 5, 6th Street Southbound: Mean Overflow Queue Length (vehicles) Cycle Time (C) equal to 60 seconds[1], Phase split (G/C) equal to 0.50

	A[2]	B[3]
Arch and 6th Street	0.0[4]	0.0[4]
Market and 6th Street	0.0[4]	0.0[4]
Chestnut and 6th Street	0.0[4]	0.0[4]

Notes:
1. Orth-Rodgers & Associates Inc., Traffic Data and Analysis: Final Report, p. 12.
2. 3 12 ft. general purpose vehicular lanes (N=3)
3. 1 12 ft. + 1 11 ft. general purpose vehicular lanes (N=2)
4. Calculated from Miller's equation, $N_{GE} = \{\exp[-1.33 * (s*G)^{1/2} * (1-x)/x]/2(1-x)$ Where s= saturation flow rate (vehicles per second), G = effective Green time, and x= the saturation ratio (=qC/sG); cited in W. Brilon and N. Wu, "Delays at Fixed-Time Traffic Signals under Time-Dependent Traffic Conditions," Traffic Engineering & Control, December 1990.

6.8. Appendix D, Measure of Impact (MOI) Sub-Analysis

This provides a crude measure of impact (MOI) of the aggregate affect of overflow conditions for the ITC during the spring weekday season, which is the peak period for visitor attendance at the INHP. It responds to the request of the NPS staff expressed during our discussions on 1/10/00. The MOI is derived from actual data collected by the traffic and site engineering consultants (TOD profile of actual bus arrival rates, sampled at each one-half hour interval; Chart 1). That is the good news. The bad news is that it is subject to the same data and methods' limitations (e.g., sample size of 1 day; assumption that same TOD profile applies to each day in the peak season). As a basis for **comparative evaluation** of the several design options, however, the crude MOI constructed may not be too bad.

Figures 7 and 8 show respectively a current and projected histogram of one-half hour intervals with bus arrival rates at each flow range.

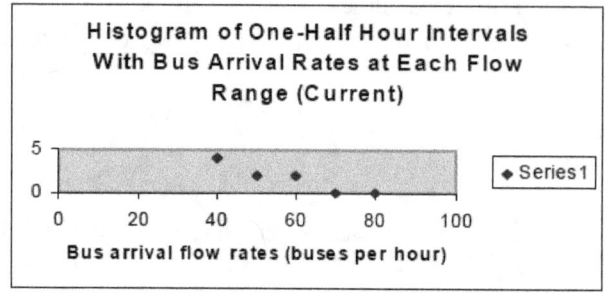

Figure 1, Source: Data from Chart 1, Orth-Rodgers et.al

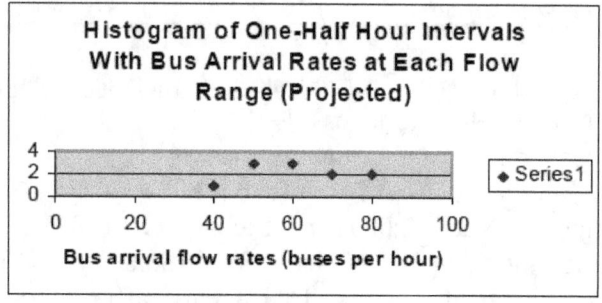

Figure 2, Source: Data from Chart 1, Orth-Rodgers et.al

The H values come directly from Figures 1 and 2 for current and projected conditions respectively, and the overflow probabilities $P(n>N|\lambda, N)$ come from the overflow probability tables in memo6_NPS.doc. The scalar value of 63 is the number of days in the peak season. The MOI crudely measures the expected number of bus arrivals during the peak season during overflow conditions (i.e., when all bus berths are occupied), given the total number of bus berths for the ITC.

Calculation of the MOI is the following:

eq. 1

$$MOI(N) = 63[H_{40}/2(P(n>N|\lambda_{40}, N) + H_{50}/2(P(n>N|\lambda_{50}, N) + H_{60}/2(P(n>N|\lambda_{60}, N) + H_{70}/2 (P(n>N|\lambda_{70}, N) + H_{80}/2(P(n>N|\lambda_{80}, N)]$$

Calculations of the MOI as a function of the number of bus berths provided (N) for both current conditions and projected conditions are given in Tables 17 and 18 respectively.

Table 6, MOI for Current Conditions

Number of Bus Berths (N)	MOI
N=11	3,339.0
N=14	548.1
N=16	75.6

Table 7, MOI for Projected Conditions

Number of Bus Berths (N)	MOI
N=11	14,080.5
N=14	6,196.0
N=16	2,368.8
N=21	100.8

Another crude measure is to construct an Index of Improvement (I^2). This measures the improvement to be gained from upgrading the ITC facility from N berths to (N+J) berths. It is calculated as the ratio of the two MOIs respectively. Tables 3 and 4 show these results for current conditions and projected conditions respectively.

Table 8, I^2 Under Current Bus Arrival conditions

Upgrade Option	I^2
N=11 to N=14	6.09
N=14 to N=16	7.25
N=11 to N=16	44.17

Table 9, I^2 Under Projected Bus Arrival conditions

Upgrade Option	I^2
N=11 to N=14	2.27
N=14 to N=16	2.61
N=16 to N=21	23.5

Summary

Several conclusions are suggested by this analysis:

- Under current peak-load bus arrival conditions, 16 bus berths (total number in combined primary bus facility and overflow facility) seems to be a minimally sufficient number to reduce to a marginal impact the occurrence of overflow events.
- Under projected bus arrival conditions (and if these conditions materialize), this number (N=16) fails. To obtain near equivalent performance (i.e., minimal overflow events), the minimally sufficient number of bus berths is 21.

Upgrading from N=14 bus berths to N=16 bus berths under current peak-load bus arrival conditions yields an enormous gain in performance of the system. Similarly, under projected peak-load bus arrival conditions, upgrading from N=16 berths to N=21 berths yields a large gain in the performance of the system.

6.9. Appendix E, Level of Service Definitions

Roadway level of services is a qualitative measure that is used to characterize operational conditions within stream, and the perception if those conditions by divers and/or passengers. Level of service on a given road is a composite measure of speed and travel time, the freedom of individual vehicles to maneuver, and the likelihood of traffic interruptions or delays. The comfort and convenience of travel and the relative safety of travel are affected by the quality of traffic flow as measured by level of service. As traffic volumes increase on a given road, congestion worsens, delays increase, and the level of service declines. The number of travel lanes, the width of the lanes, the presence of usable road shoulders, the roadway grade, and the mix of traffic all influence level of service.

Six levels of service are defined in the 1994 Highway Capacity Manual for several types of roadway facilities. The levels of service are given letter designations, from A to F, with level of service A representing the best operating conditions and level of service F the worst. The service levels apply to typical operating conditions. Accidents, weather, road conditions, and other incidents (such as delays for viewing the park) are not addressed by the level of service measures. The impacts of incidents or degraded road conditions on traffic flow are greater for the lower level of service ranges of operation.

The following definitions have been developed for each level of service for continuous roadways.

- *Level of Service A* – represents free flow. Individual users are virtually unaffected by the presence of others on the road. Nearly all drivers are free to select their desired speeds and to maneuver within the traffic stream. The general level of comfort and convenience provided to the motorist, passenger, or pedestrian is excellent.

- *Level of Service B* – represents high quality, stable traffic flow. The presence of other users in the traffic stream begins to be noticeable to individual drivers. The freedom to select desired speeds is relatively high but there is a slight decline in the freedom to maneuver within the traffic stream from level of service A. The level of comfort and convenience provided to individual travelers is somewhat less than at level of service A, because the presence of others in the traffic stream begins to affect individual behavior.

- *Level of Service C* – marks the beginning of the range of traffic flow in which the travel of individual users becomes significantly affected by other vehicles in the traffic stream. The selection of speed by most users is affected by the presence of other vehicles. Maneuvering within the traffic stream requires substantial vigilance on the part of the driver. The general level of comfort and convenience declines noticeably at this level.

- *Level of Service D –* represents the upper end of traffic volumes that can be accommodated while maintaining stable traffic flow. Vehicle speeds and the freedom to maneuver are severely restricted for nearly all users. Drivers and pedestrians experience a generally poor level of comfort and convenience.

- *Level of Service E –* represents operating conditions at or near the capacity of the roadway. All speeds are reduced to a low, but relatively uniform value. Freedom to maneuver within the traffic stream is virtually non-existent, and maneuvers require drivers to force vehicles or pedestrians to "give way." Comfort and convenience levels are extremely poor, and driver or pedestrian frustration is generally high. Operations at this level are usually unstable, because small increases in flow or minor disruptions within the traffic stream will cause all traffic to stop.

- *Level of Service F –* is used to define forced flow. Level of service F occurs when more traffic attempts to use a road segment than the capacity of the segment. Long queues form in the traffic stream. Operations within the queues are characterized by stop-and-go waves, and flow is extremely unstable. Vehicles may progress at reasonable speeds for several hundred feet or more, then be required to stop on a cyclic fashion. Comfort and convenience are extremely poor and drivers may become frustrated.